The Politics of Representation

The Democratic Convention 1972

. . . .

DENIS G. SULLIVAN
JEFFREY L. PRESSMAN
BENJAMIN I. PAGE
JOHN J. LYONS

St. Martin's Press, New York

Library of Congress Catalog Card Number: 73-88804
Copyright © 1974 by St. Martin's Press, Inc.
All Rights Reserved.
Manufactured in the United States of America.
For information, write: St. Martin's Press, Inc.,
175 Fifth Avenue, New York, N.Y. 10010

AFFILIATED PUBLISHERS: Macmillan Limited, London—
also at Bombay, Calcutta, Madras, and Melbourne.

The illustration on p. iv is reprinted by permission of
Time/Life Picture Agency.

To Mrs. Selma Rubin and the staff of the Blue Waters Hotel for their thoughtful attention to our needs

"I understand the new politics now—they're in an' we're out."

Preface

The idea for this study emerged in the spring of 1972 from a series of conversations stimulated by our joint teaching of the introductory course on American Government at Dartmouth College. We were wrestling intellectually with the problems of political nominating conventions. We perceived that the McGovern-Fraser Commission reforms, coupled with the McGovern candidacy for the nomination, would bring significant changes in delegate selection and other decision procedures at the 1972 Democratic convention; and we supposed that the changes would put to a severe test the traditional wisdom concerning the functions and dynamics of national party nominating conventions in general.

The idea for a study turned quickly into a proposal for students and faculty from Dartmouth to travel to Miami and interview delegates over the course of the convention. And so on July 7, three days before the opening gavel on Monday night, a student-faculty group boarded a plane in Boston for Miami International Airport.

All of this was made possible by support from a number of different sources. Basic support was provided through a generous grant from the Ford Foundation, and special thanks go to William Grinker of the Foundation who was so helpful at every stage of our proposal. Professor Frank Smallwood and Thomas Davis, through a grant from the Dartmouth Public Affairs Center, provided travel, food, and lodging expenses for the initial student group. Because the project was attractive to so many students at Dartmouth, Dartmouth College President John G. Kemeny provided additional funds so that we could increase the number of students who could travel to Miami.

To our interviewers in Miami—Robert Bachelder, Eric Easterly, William Emmons, Alfred Frawley, David Hoeh, Sandy Hoeh, Michael Hollis, Charles Johnson, Gerald Johnson, Ernie Kessler, Galen Kirkland, John Lamond, John Lyons, Michael Marohn, Peter McKeever, Joost Van Nispen, Geoffrey Parker, Kate Pressman, Charles Schudson, Karen Schudson, Susan Smallwood, Judy Soisson, Thomas Watkin, Andrea Wolfman, and Bruce Westcott—we express thanks for a job well done.

Lucille Flanders of the Dartmouth Public Affairs Center served as our secretary in Hanover, and Charlotte Guarino did the same while we were in Miami. Both proved indispensable. Some of our students doubled as interviewers and observers of particular state delegations: Kate Pressman on Connecticut; Charles Johnson, John Lamond, and Ernie Kessler on Massachusetts; and John Lyons on New Hampshire. Although our study does not deal with specific state delegations, the reports of these students were quite useful in shaping our thoughts about the relationship between state delegations and candidate organizations.

Two students should be singled out because of their special contributions. John Lyons was at the center of our project from its inception to its conclusion. He was responsible for drawing the sample, assisting in the construction of the questionnaire, preparing the data for the computer, and contributing a chapter to our report. Geoffrey Parker performed the onerous but vitally important task of coding the interview data into a computer-readable form with extraordinary skill and persistence. He was assisted by Jeffrey Merritt and Charles Johnson. The reliability of their work was gratifyingly high. The statistical analysis was greatly facilitated through the use of Dartmouth College's Project IMPRESS. Finally, our thanks go to our typists, Lucille E. Flanders and Virginia Ord Church.

The authors are happy to take full responsibility for this book; neither Dartmouth College nor the Ford Foundation shares any of the responsibility for its contents.

Denis G. Sullivan   Jeffrey L. Pressman   Benjamin I. Page

Dartmouth College   Hanover, New Hampshire   May 18, 1973

Contents

chapter one
Four Dilemmas in Representation   1

Demands for Change, 1968-1972   3
Representation   10
Arenas of Decision Making at the Convention   11
Issue Voting and the Making of a Platform   13
Political Style   14

chapter two
The Impact of Reform on Representation   17

Group Representation and Political Experience   23
Issue Opinions—1972   30
Conclusion: Goals and Consequences of Representation   34

chapter three
Arenas of Decision: Innovation in Group Representation at the Convention   41

The Convention Examined: Recreation Versus Work   43
Focus on Arenas   44
Organizational Problems of the Caucus   58
The Many Functions of State Delegations   62
The Importance of Candidate Organizations   64
Conclusions   65

chapter four

Innovation and Compromise: The Making of a Party Platform 71

Does It Matter? 71
What Did It Say? 78
How Did It Come About? 91
Conclusion: What Did It All Mean? 112

chapter five

Winners and Losers: The Impact of Power on Purism and Professionalism 116

The Effects of Winning and Losing on Political Purism 119
The Stability of Political Style—a Test 122
Losers and Legitimation 127

appendix a

Sampling Procedure 135

appendix b

Questionnaire 139

appendix c

Chronology of Convention Events 147

Index 151

chapter one

Four Dilemmas in Representation

What follows in this book is not just an account of a particular nominating convention; it goes beyond the particulars of the Democratic convention in Miami to examine some of the more enduring dilemmas that found expression in the events of spring and summer 1972.

A central problem in any democratic society involves what Harold Lasswell has termed an "empowering process." That is, the process by which political parties select leaders whom they can support and who are capable of mounting successful electoral campaigns. But political parties, like other organizations, face a number of dilemmas when they attempt to formulate optimal selection procedures. The ways in which these dilemmas were faced in the period of 1968 to 1972, and what the tentative solutions revealed about the nature of the political process, constitute the core of this book.

The first dilemma arises from the issue of deciding who is entitled to participate directly in the nomination process. Even this basic problem involves complex issues. Not all citizens who declare themselves in support of a candidate can be considered members of that candidate's party. Yet, who is to decide where the boundary between member and supporter lies? Party membership in the United States seems to be had for the asking. Political parties are not private organizations that can easily refuse freely offered services. Moreover, in periods of dissatisfaction with political parties, amateur activists often demand that the scope of participation in the parties be widened to include them. The issue of participation, then, creates a natural tension between the more professional politician and the amateur activist. The result of the tension that developed in 1968 was a broadening of opportunities for participation in 1972, an experiment in which the mix of amateur activists and professionals would be altered.

The second dilemma is, in one sense, a consequence of the first. If the convention organization of a party receives an infusion of new delegates whose loyalties may be to interests outside the party, as well as to those within the party, how will these outside interests receive representation? Delegates with primary loyalties to labor, southerners, women, blacks, the elderly, the young will vote and decide issues in company with those whose loyalties focus on the party. The new delegates may think of themselves as directly representing outside interests and may desire their own convention sites to provide symbolic recognition of their group's importance; they may also want candidates to appear before their groups and to respond directly to the interests they represent.

Their presence gives rise to a third dilemma—the relationship between issue goals and the survival of a party as an organization. Parties have to decide where their priorities lie. In their choice of leaders and platforms they may indicate a responsiveness to what has been "tried and true"—to the nurturance of old constituencies—or they might look to new constituencies with new issue orientations. And parties may, in their platform and choice of leaders, contribute to the development of new constituencies in exchange for new support. In this sense, then, a party becomes educative; its platform can show where the party might go, as well as where it has been. The dilemma is, of course, characteristic of all organizations: as their political environments change, or seem to change, parties run the risk of losing the old while attracting the new.

Finally, there is the central dilemma of all politics—the balance between issue purity and organizational power. Parties are organizations that must attract votes to survive. Yet they also exist as instruments to achieve issue goals. Awareness of this dilemma on the part of a party's members creates a profound organizational tension. Periodically, the tension comes to be expressed in the conflict between the professional politician and the issue purist, the latter willing to sacrifice power for integrity, and the former, integrity for power. Over time, however, the tension seems to be resolved through the imperatives of organizational power driving out or transforming the issue purists. Thus, the survival of issue concern may well depend on fresh infusions of personnel whose incentives for participation are directly related to important new issues.

Each dilemma we have described was heightened by the events between 1968 and 1972. In extreme form, it seemed as if the changes during this period had tilted the balance so that the new would be emphasized at the expense of the old, direct representation at the expense of indirect, innovation at the expense of tradition, and issue purity at the expense of political professionalism. But conventional wisdom extolled the old, indirect representation, responsiveness to traditional constituencies, and issue pragmatism. Each of the following chapters examines how one of the above dilemmas was resolved in the Democratic Presidential Nominating Convention of 1972.

Demands for Change, 1968–1972

In 1968 the Democratic party was in the throes of adjusting to the demands of groups with newly won power positions in American politics. Although the party thought of itself as representing those who demanded change in society, spokesmen for the groups most concerned with change did not agree. From the perspective of many blacks in America, the Democratic party was basically white. For women, the party was predominantly male.[1] And for the young, the party was in the hands of the old.[2]

Because these charges appeared to be true, and because on a variety of issues in American society blacks differed from whites, males from females, and young from old, the new power groups believed that the middle-aged, white, male regulars who exercised disproportionate control in the party would never understand nor accept their needs and aspirations. For some, then, the party needed reform, and the reform could only move in one direction. Distrust of the regulars by leaders of new power groupings led to a demand for direct representation in the policy-making procedures of the party.

Only by such a move could the party regain its legitimacy among those it professed to represent.

Traditionally, group demands have been filtered through the party apparatus on local, state, and national levels. Representation has been indirect—the responsibility of those who have made politics a lifelong commitment and who view themselves as professionals. The demand for direct representation was thus a challenge to the legitimacy of an old profession. Along with the desire for direct representation there were demands that the traditional style of politics be altered to reflect new issues and thus a "new politics." For many members of the new groups, issues really did matter, and parties became instruments for their expression. Demands for changes in representation were joined with a new political style; the ideal was an issue-oriented party that would articulate its conceptions of justice.

Before going further, it should be pointed out that grouping together youth, blacks, and women—as if they all bear the same relation to the Democratic party—is somewhat misleading. Their differences may be more instructive than their similarities. By any measure, the success of the Democratic coalition on the national level has been more dependent upon the continuing support of blacks than of women or youth. Black loyalty to the Democratic party, a product of the 1930s depression and the emergence of a class-based politics, was strengthened in the 1960s by the civil-rights movement. Many southern blacks, coming to the polls for the first time in the 1960s, expressed loyalty to the Democrats in both sentiment and behavior. From 1960 to 1968, as Figure 1 shows, black loyalty to the Democratic party surged at a time when Democratic loyalty was declining nationally.

In 1968, then, the Democratic party had established a clear partisan advantage among blacks, and blacks were contributing substantially to the Democratic party's electoral successes. Robert Axelrod has calculated that in terms of a percentage contribution to the party's electoral success in Presidential elections, the contribution of blacks rose from an average of 6 percent in the 1950s to 19 percent in 1968.[3] Yet in the 1968 Democratic Nominating Convention only 5 percent of the delegates were black. How significant this discrepancy may

FIGURE 1.

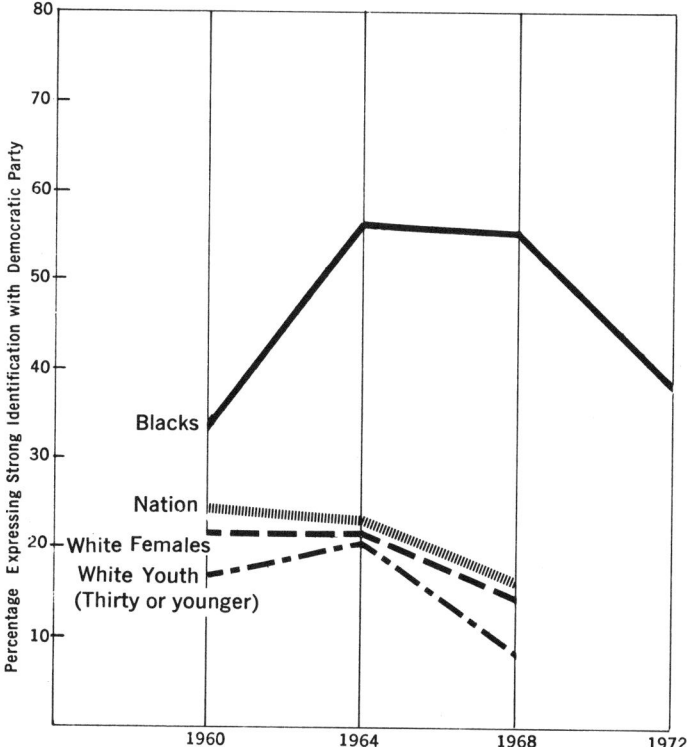

Percentages of Expressions of Strong Party Loyalty Toward the Democratic Party Between 1960 and October 1972

Source: ICPR prior to 1972. See Note 4 for question wording. The 1972 percentage for blacks was provided by Arthur Miller, et al, *Social Conflict and Political Estrangement, 1958-72*, delivered at the 1972 Midwest Political Science Association Meeting. Data are not yet available for the other groups.

prove to be cannot be answered here. Suffice it to say that it could not help the Democrats maintain their partisan advantage among blacks and, in fact, it may hurt them. Figure 1 shows another large shift among blacks in the Democratic party; in this case a 16 percent reduction in the percentage of blacks who identify strongly with the party. The reasons for this are as yet obscure, but it may well be that the increase in black representation at the 1972 Democratic National Convention will dampen the shift.

Although women and youth were also underrepresented in

the 1968 convention, they were not, in the sense the blacks were, real political groups with identifiable interests. Contrary to popular opinion, the young in the 1960s were by no means united in their opposition to the Vietnam war. In fact, youth as a group was slightly less dovish on the war than was the general population. Nor were young people in agreement on economic and social policy. Their views were slightly more liberal than those of their elders, but the differences between the opinions of the age groups were mainly ones of degree. Again, Figure 1 is instructive in this regard; although the decline in the percentage of those under thirty who identified strongly with the Democratic party is substantial, it simply mirrors national trends. It would be an exaggeration to view this drift away from the Democrats on the part of the young as a distinct alienation; rather, there seems to be a secular trend away from strong party identification for all groups except blacks.[4]

The emergence of the political power of women toward the end of the 1960s raises yet another issue. It was only after 1968 that women began to organize effectively for political action and to demand representation in the councils of the party in relation to their numbers in the population. The issues dividing men and women had not been sharply felt within the party system by 1968, and, thus, the changes in strength of party loyalty among women in the 1960s closely parallel the national trend. For women, and to a lesser extent for youth, the Democratic party was only one of many institutions to which they had been denied access.

For blacks, however, the case was more powerful. They did not need to rest their argument on the issue of societal justice; they had a concrete political claim to increased representation. The party needed them. But distinctions among the claims of the three groups were submerged in the rhetoric of the McGovern Commission report. Spokesmen for women, blacks, and youth were able to argue quite effectively that the Democratic party could not long remain their representative unless members of each group participated directly in party decision-making processes. The persuasiveness of the argument, and its political utility to the McGovern organization, did have far-

Four Dilemmas in Representation 7

reaching implications for the classic model of convention decision making.

The classic model assumes the existence of competition among candidate organizations for the support of convention delegates who are party activists. The salient roles are *party member* and *convention delegate*. The great importance of party goals to the average delegate has been pointed out by Nelson Polsby and Aaron Wildavsky: "The major goals of most delegates to national conventions may be simply described: to nominate a man who can win the election; to unify the party; to obtain some claim on the nominee; and to strengthen state party organizations." [5] In the classic model of convention decision making, delegates pursue these goals through state delegations that, operating as cohesive units, bargain with each other and with candidate organizations. The rank-and-file delegates attach themselves to hierarchical leaders who have major roles in national, state, or local party organizations. The average delegate's concern with winning an election drives him to consider supporting candidates who can harness the short-term forces to his party. Thus, in 1952, regular Republicans might have found Eisenhower's political inexperience distasteful, but they could support him because they recognized a winner. But the party activist delegate does not want to sacrifice the long-term base of his party for short-term gains. Thus, he must test each candidate against the standard of party unity: Can the candidate draw together the various constituencies of the party?

The McGovern-Fraser reforms, it was said, would change the *structure of the convention,* the *nature of the delegates,* and *group representation* in ways that would limit the relevance of the classic model. These three changes are, of course, related. For purposes of illustration, let us make a hypothetical examination of the issue of integration, or unity, of state delegations at the 1972 convention. One of the most important changes in convention structure—the abolition of the unit rule —would diminish the importance of hierarchical state delegation leaders as members of the bargaining arena. Controlling a majority of the state delegates no longer assured a state delegation leader of all the votes allocated to the state. Thus minority forces within the delegation would be sought out by candidate organizations attempting to fashion winning coalitions. The abolition of the unit rule and the reduction of the importance of state party leaders in state delegations would multiply the number of groups to be consulted in forming coalitions and strain an already burdened information system. There would be strong incentives to find ways to assemble the smaller groups into more manageable bargaining units.

The desire, and need, to develop new kinds of bargaining units would find expression in new patterns of group representation at the convention. With the increase in the number of women, youths, and blacks, and nonparty activists of all kinds, state delegations would be subject to even more factionalization than might be predicted by the abolition of the unit rule. Thus, the possibility might arise that interest-group representation at the convention would go beyond the platform-committee fights and labor-union activity.

If such a development did occur, it would threaten the autonomy of the convention as a decision-making system with its own boundaries and procedures. The autonomy of the convention is traditionally symbolized by prohibiting nondelegates from entering the convention floor and, in addition, by a number of devices designed to heighten the salience of the delegate role. Party symbols are paraded before the delegates who learn to perceive their roles in a party-related frame of reference, but these devices may now be far less effective in promoting concern for party-related goals than they have been in the past. The McGovern-Fraser Reform Commission recommendations concerning open caucuses, minority-group representation, and so forth, pose another threat to convention autonomy because they allow for a larger number of nonparty group appeals than had come from delegates at past conventions—a development that would reduce integration within the state delegations and transform the bargaining arena.

It was thought, too, that symbolic aspects of representation might be involved. The increase in nonparty activists and minority-group representation at the convention meant that large numbers of local and state party officials had been displaced from their positions within state delegations. Although they "represented" the party in an organizational sense, they were in Miami—if indeed they came to Miami—as nondelegates. In some sense, then, a substantial part of the "normal" party had been turned out of its own house by nonparty activists. This development would diminish the legitimacy of the convention output if it went against the grain of the loyalists.

Along with a decline in state delegation integration, there would be an increase in openly expressed conflict within and between delegations. The Wallace, Humphrey, and McGovern organizations would challenge the very basic beliefs each had about its own members and about members of the other two candidate organizations. The challenges would result in a sharp rise in ethnocentric political thinking. Not only would this be a natural result of diversity at the convention but it would be fueled by the newness of many delegates to the game of politics.

Such a scenario could have been adequately tested if the nomination had been contested. But in 1972, uncertainty as to the nominee was virtually eliminated by the Monday-night vote on the California credentials challenge. Still, there were important tasks before the convention that would test the decision-making power of the new groups and the ability of the party to unify itself around its candidate and platform. And the challenge to the old politics would still raise significant questions about a political theory of representation, convention decision making, the importance of platform issues in democratic theory, and, finally, matters of political style.

Our research in dealing with these questions was based upon (1) first-hand observation of caucuses, state delegation meetings, and convention floor proceedings, (2) structured interviews in Miami with a randomly selected sample of 234 delegates over the five-day period of the convention, and (3) the results of a preconvention CBS poll of all delegates. Our interviews were administered by Dartmouth students and faculty in the lobbies of hotels where delegates were staying, in coffee shops and restaurants, and just off the convention floor. Each interviewer had a schedule of questions. (A copy of the interview schedule is reproduced in Appendix B.) Some of the questions were quite structured; others were more open-ended and allowed delegates a chance to speak at length about their hopes and fears. The students turned out to be superb interviewers and displayed unflagging energy in seeking out delegates. Now let us turn to a brief summary of our findings.

Representation

In Chapter 2, John Lyons and Denis Sullivan examine the effects of the McGovern-Fraser Reform Commission rule changes on patterns of representation at the convention.[6] Their analysis reveals that the successes and failures of convention reform in 1972 cannot be divorced from the impact of the short-term forces propelling McGovern to a position of leadership in the party. If the country is to benefit from the experience of 1972, it must learn not to confound the effects of the reform rules with the effects of a successful insurgent candidate on the composition of convention delegates. When McGovern went to Miami, a near-majority of the convention delegates was already committed to him through state conventions and primaries. Without doubt, the new rules on primaries and state conventions made it easier for McGovern to win delegates, but it would be folly to impute such powerful effects to formal rules alone. Muskie and Humphrey had relatively weak candidate organizations; McGovern supporters prior to the convention were intense and well organized.

The extent to which the 1972 convention was more unrepresentative of rank-and-file Democrats than the 1968 convention was due as much to McGovern's success in capturing state conventions and primaries as to the quota system. Lyons and Sullivan argue that holding the so-called quota system responsible for the "radicalization" of the convention is, at best, misleading and, at worst, false. To understand why such a proposition gains currency, one must understand that such assertions have political functions; to act as if the assertion is true may affect the distribution of power within the party. Its political function seems to be (1) to discredit spokesmen for the new constituencies as radical and, as a consequence, without support in their groups, and (2) to signal the old constituencies, such as the party-labor and blue-collar groups, that they are returning to positions of leadership within the party.

For these twin purposes it becomes convenient to attribute a variety of the party's current ailments to the quota system.[7]

Arenas of Decision Making at the Convention

In the classic model of convention decision making, party activists gather to filter candidates in terms of their issue positions, acceptability to all segments of the party, and capacity to conduct a winning campaign in November. The legitimacy of this model came into question because it had denied access to significant new groups and was thus incapable of articulating their interests. The solution, according to opinion leaders within these groups, was a kind of direct representation and new modes of convention decision procedure.

In Chapter 3, Jeffrey Pressman looks at the relative success of the new modes of convention participation against the backdrop of old-style candidate organizations and state delegations. Pressman's answer to the question of the viability of new modes of representation is that traditional convention politics —working through candidate organizations and state delegations—reasserted itself as the convention wore on. Participation in the functional caucuses—of blacks, women, the young— dwindled over the five-day period.

Pressman points out that the structure of the convention decision-making process, the ways in which the delegates were selected, and the overlap between membership in group caucuses and support for McGovern made it difficult for the caucuses to exert an independent effect on convention outcomes.

Those who had high hopes for blacks, women, and the young must remember that most caucus participants were selected by candidate organizations in their own states or districts to run pledged or supporting a candidate. Delegates, by and large, came to Miami supporting a candidate as their first order of business and, only secondarily, representing a group goal. This was especially true for McGovern delegates. The delegates, excluding for the moment the Wallacites, were most strongly committed to their candidates for issue-related reasons. And the issue orientations of McGovern delegates were the same as those of the leadership of the three large caucus efforts. Thus, the natural pool available to develop a power structure independent of candidate organizations was the pool most strongly committed to McGovern. The only chance for caucus power—among blacks, women, or the young —would have been the growth of the perception on the part of McGovern supporters that their candidate could not win the nomination. The driving force for the extraordinary self-restraint and discipline shown by McGovern delegates during the credentials challenges on Monday night was the delegates' believe that, by subordinating issue preferences, the McGovern organization would stay unified and produce a convention winner by Wednesday evening.

Pressman's conclusions raise questions of a more fundamental sort concerning the conditions for effective representation of the interests of groups such as women, the young, and blacks. We have already pointed out the significance of the expectation that McGovern was going to win the nomination. But the whole issue of representation, at least as we have spoken of it so far, presupposes some homogeneity of interest within the group that seeks representation. This was not the case for the three relevant interest groups in 1972. As Pressman points out, black delegates fresh from the first National Black Political Convention held at Gary, Indiana, competed with the more conservative Congressional Black Caucus for leadership of the Black Caucus. Effective group action at a convention spanning five days requires prior coordination and agreement, conditions that were met only by the candidate organizations. The difficulties faced by blacks proved even greater for youth and women. Indeed, the youth caucus seems hardly to have gotten off the ground.

It is possible, of course, that if McGovern had fallen short of a majority and the expectation of victory had declined among his supporters, the caucuses might have become power centers. Whether this development would have further increased the rifts in each caucus, or whether it would possibly have unified them, we cannot tell. The same reasoning we applied to the unity of the McGovern organization would perhaps apply here. A deadlocked convention would increase the relative power of caucus groups. Caucus members, realizing their potential power and scenting the possibility of achiev-

Issue Voting and the Making of a Platform

Benjamin Page, in his discussion in Chapter 4 of the platform and the role of issues, goes beyond the confines of the convention proceedings in Miami to include an analysis of the drafting of the platform by the Platform Committee in the late spring of 1972. The drama, that was to be replayed on the convention floor, involved a revolt by some of the more issue-oriented McGovern supporters on the Platform Committee against the pragmatic orientations of both the Democratic regulars and the McGovern organization leadership.

As Page points out, the conflict there presaged a strongly issue-oriented convention in Miami. But one of the more interesting findings in Page's account is that a strong issue orientation does not invariably lead to a desire to write a platform in one's own issue image (although, as Page points out, one-quarter of the McGovern delegates thought the platform very important as either an instrument to attract issue-oriented voters or as a forum for the expression of correct issue positions). Yet, the Wallace organization, having no chance to win and being the candidate organization with the highest percentage of amateurs, took the platform very seriously. Over one-third of the Wallacites thought it was important that the platform express the correct issue positions, and 83 percent thought that the antibusing plank, the issue that mattered most to them, should be included. Compare this, for example, with McGovern delegate response to the plank calling for the U.S. withdrawal from Vietnam; little more than one-quarter expressly stated in response to our interviewers' queries that it should be included in the platform.

The key to this seeming puzzle lay in the refusal of the McGovern supporters to think of the platform and issue orientation as synonymous. For the McGovernites who did group these two considerations together, the compulsion was strong to have the platform express the correct issue position. A good test case is the issue of guaranteed annual income, which a strong majority of the delegates favored and the society in general opposed. Considering only delegates who favored the issue, 6 percent of those who thought a platform should be designed to attract votes wanted it included as a plank; of those who thought a platform should express the correct issue position, however, the percentage that wanted it included was 35. So if the McGovern delegates were issue oriented, and there is overwhelming evidence that they were, their view of the secondary importance of the platform allowed them to behave in a reasonably instrumental fashion.

Political Style

In Chapter 5, Denis Sullivan deals with the significance of what has come to be called "the new political style"—the style of the purist, as opposed to that of the traditional politician. Before it became clear that McGovern had the support of a majority of the delegates, many people believed that the convention would be filled with amateur purists supporting candidates such as Wallace and McGovern. If the convention did indeed turn out to be one in which bargaining took place, it was thought that the purist delegates would be poorly equipped to participate and would not yield gracefully to discipline imposed from above.

The purists would view the convention not as an arena for bargaining and coalition-building, but rather as a stage for presenting to themselves and to others an intense commitment to a candidate or an ideology. For the purist, "rationality" would mean strategies, not only for displaying commitment, but also for capturing public attention, bolstering group morale, and showing the opposition what purists really were like.

The professionals, on the other hand, would display a willingness to consider bargaining, trade-offs, and the like. They would see their votes as a scarce resource. Though not without commitment to candidate or ideology, they would be willing to measure their commitment against other alternatives. The presumption was that they would use their votes and other resources at the convention in a way that would further their policy goals.

Although the convention did not allow us to examine the clash of political styles in ways we had anticipated, it did lead us to an important finding. As Sullivan argues, purism as a political style is not independent of winning and losing. It turns out that it is quite rational for losers to become purists, especially when they perceive that the party is being captured by an insurgent group. What seemed to have happened during the course of the convention, according to Sullivan, was that the frustration of the Democratic regulars expressed itself in an increasingly purist political style. Sullivan had also hypothesized that winning might have increased the pragmatic orientation of the McGovern supporters, but this did not seem to be the case. The winners were as issue purist at the end of the convention, when they had captured the party, as they were before coming to Miami.

NOTES

1. I have purposely overstated the case to give the reader some sense of the rhetoric. I suspect the worry about the lack of representation is exaggerated in the first paragraph.

2. As we point out in Chapter 2, only 6 percent of the delegates in 1968 were black, 2 percent were under thirty, and 14 percent were women.

3. Robert Axelrod, "Where the Votes Come From: An Analysis of Electoral Coalitions, 1952–1968," *American Political Science Review*, vol. 66, no. 1 (March 1972): 11–20. The measure is a simple one that includes the size of the group, its turnout in the election, and percentage of its vote cast for the party as compared with national turnout and the percentage of the national vote cast for the party.

4. The question asked of each citizen in the University of Michigan Survey Research Center sample reads as follows, "Generally speaking, do you usually think of yourself as a Republican, a Democrat, an Independent, or what? . . . Would you call yourself a strong (R) (D)?" There was, in the 1960s, a slight decline in the percentage identifying with party and, thus, a rise in the percentage that was independent. Again white youth led the pack, rising from 10 percent Independent in 1960 to around 50 percent in 1968. Women paralleled the national trend, while blacks showed no change.

5. Nelson W. Polsby and Aaron Wildavsky, "Uncertainty and Decision Making at the National Convention," *Western Political Quarterly*, vol. 13, no. 3 (September 1960): 609–19.

6. We appreciate the kindness of CBS, and especially of Milton Konofsky at CBS who supervised the data gathering at Miami, for making it available to our project. In attempting to make the relevant comparisons, we faced some difficult problems. There are no data on issue preferences of the 1968 delegates; only on what issues the delegates thought important. In 1972, on the other hand, there are data on what the delegates thought about some issues but no data on Democratic party rank and filers. The latter problem presents few difficulties; data will eventually be available from the Survey Research Center at Michigan.

7. See, for example, the draft version of the Coalition for a Democratic Majority Task Force Report on the McGovern-Fraser Guidelines, *Towards Fairness and Unity for '76*, May 1973.

chapter two

The Impact of Reform on Representation

INTERVIEWER: What do you think of the new rules for delegate selection?
DELEGATE 1: "I wouldn't be here without them. . . ."
DELEGATE 2: "McGovern is a bastard . . . changed the rules to suit his own candidacy."[1]

One need not be Sherlock Holmes to infer correctly that Delegate 1 was a McGovern supporter who felt that she and her candidate had been benefited by the reform rules for delegate selection in 1972. Delegate 2 expressed a common theme among regular Democrats at the convention; that somehow the rules changes had disadvantaged their candidates, and that those changes could also be blamed for the absence of many of their best friends. From the perspectives of both the McGovern and anti-McGovern people, the new rules were closely tied to the candidacy of George McGovern. And in the bathos of defeat in November 1972, the reform rules became a lightning rod for the myriad failures of the Democratic party. In the mind's eye of the average Democrat, the reforms and defeat were nearly synonymous.[2]

The Democratic party reform rules had two sharply different but important aspects. The now-famous group quota provision specified that blacks, women, and youth be represented in each state delegation in "reasonable relationship to their presence" in the population of each state. But possibly more important was a change in the procedures for local-caucus and state-convention delegate selection. In 1972, roughly one-third of all delegates would be elected in state conventions, yet party regulars had long been accused of controlling state conventions to suit their own purposes. The rules in 1972 specified a number of changes that would open local caucuses and state conventions to much broader participation by non-party regulars.[3]

In the postelection period of 1972, the group quota provisions were subjected to severe attacks by regular party groups who felt shut out during the 1972 convention. Even George McGovern, a leader in the reform movement, backed off from reform in his testimony before a spring 1972 meeting of a new party Charter Commission on delegate selection rules for the 1976 convention. McGovern advocated the removal of the phrase "reasonable relationship to their presence" in the population of each state, which would, in effect, abolish the group quota provision. In addition, McGovern modified his position on the procedural openness provisions by supporting what amounted to a quota for senior party leaders and asking for increased control by candidate organizations over delegates pledged to a candidate.[4]

The argument on the effects of the party reform rules has two sharply different aspects. The argument against the quota provision assumes that candidate organizations will be unable to find enough blacks, youth, and women with political experience comparable to delegates who are displaced by the quotas. The second argument, attacking the open procedure reforms, suggests that opening local-district caucuses and state conventions to participation by nonregular Democrats would facilitate an insurgent candidacy based on issue-oriented, politically inexperienced, youthful supporters. The reforms, then, might result in a successful insurgent candidacy in state conventions against the wishes of those who had traditionally controlled the conventions—the party regulars.[5]

Both arguments misrepresent the effects of convention reform—principally, the radicalization of the delegates and their lack of political experience. As we shall try to show in some detail later, the composition of the delegates at Miami in 1972—both in terms of issue opinions and political experience—reflected in large measure the McGovern insurgency whose prospects for success were only marginally affected by the new reform rules.

The image of McGovern fanatics running roughshod over party regulars in state conventions is simply not supported by the facts. The bulk of McGovern's support came from his victories in primary elections. Over 51 percent of the delegates elected in primaries supported McGovern, while the combined opposition of Humphrey-Muskie-Jackson received only 21 percent.[6] Thus, McGovern was a typical insurgent in the sense that he established his base in the more open forum provided by the primary elections. The picture is somewhat different when we turn to delegates selected by state conventions. In 1972 there were roughly 1,009 delegates selected in state conventions, approximately one-third of all regular delegates. The new rules on open procedures surely helped McGovern in wresting delegates away from party regulars who wanted to travel to Miami uncommitted or supporting a party regular candidate. And in some cases, amateur McGovernites did replace local and state party leaders on state delegations. But as Figure 1 shows, the new rules on procedures and group quotas did not result in McGovern's domination of state conventions: by June 3, 1972, McGovern held only a slight edge in support among delegates elected in state conventions. Even though his margin of support increased throughout June, the difference by convention time was not large; McGovern was supported by 32 percent of state convention delegates, while 20 percent supported Muskie, Humphrey, or Jackson. Following the top line in Figure 1, which traces the growth of delegate support in primary elections, it appears that the narrow McGovern victory in the California winner-take-all primary (271 votes) on June 6 accelerated McGovern's inroads into state convention delegates.[7]

It might be more useful to consider other factors that would explain McGovern's nomination success and electoral failure than look longingly at the reform rules. The factors seem remarkably similar to those propelling Goldwater to the Republican nomination in 1964. Both Goldwater and McGovern were insurgents seeking their party's nomination to run against strong and popular White House incumbents. The Republicans in 1964, like the Democrats in 1972, were given little chance

FIGURE 1.

Delegate and Rank-and-File Support for Leading Democratic Candidates

a. Cumulative Percentage Among Delegates

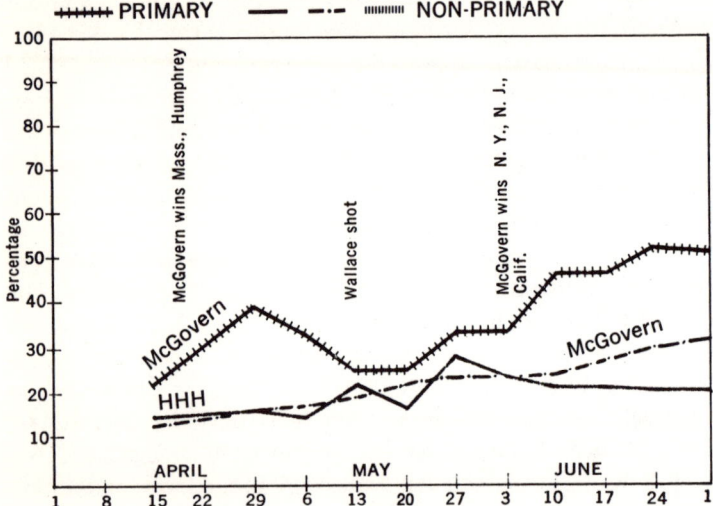

b. Percentage Among Democratic Rank and File — Public Opinion Polls

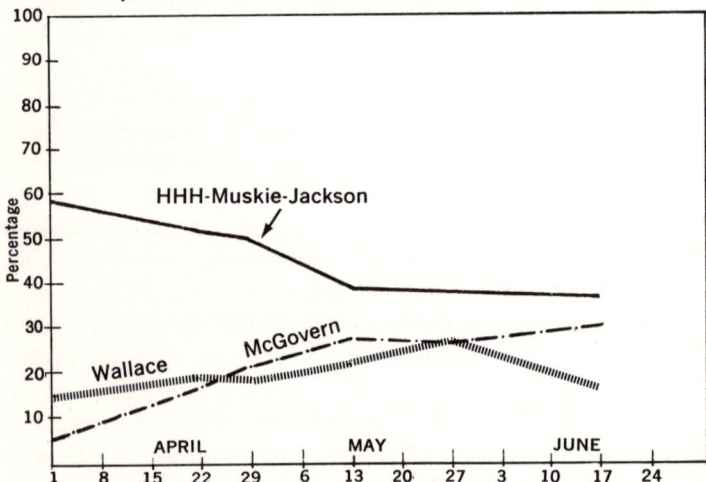

Source: Delegate data from *National Journal* April 15 through July 1, 1972. Public opinion data from Gallup Opinion Index with the exception of a May 9-10 Harris Poll including Independents as well as Democrats. Gallup question reads as follows: "Which one of the men on this list would you like to see nominated as the Democratic candidate for President in 1972?"

of regaining the White House regardless of the character of their nominee. Perhaps this expectation of defeat in November made the regulars a little less intense in their opposition to the insurgencies of Goldwater and McGovern. Moreover, both 1964 and 1972 demonstrated the capriciousness of politics. Rockefeller, the leading centrist opponent of Goldwater in 1964, was politically crippled as a consequence of his divorce and remarriage during the campaign year. And Ted Kennedy—probably the leading Democratic candidate in 1972—was not only waiting for a more propitious year in which to announce his candidacy; his political reputation had suffered a sharp blow as a result of the Chappaquiddick incident.

The similarities go beyond the above background factors. Both Goldwater and McGovern had mixed receptions in the primaries. Both candidates used primaries as devices for pyramiding their power in order to capture state convention delegates. Both had groups of intense followers who used their superior organizational capacity to penetrate delegate selection processes at the state conventions.

But there were differences between the McGovern and Goldwater insurgencies. Goldwater did far better in state conventions than did McGovern. And McGovern gained in public opinion polls while Goldwater barely held his own.[8] But perhaps a more important difference is that Goldwater was the only insurgent in 1964. In 1972, the Wallace candidacy, although cut short by the attempted assassination, had a profound effect in the preconvention period. Although Figure 1-a does not show it, Wallace was gaining in delegate strength, from 13 percent on April 29 to 27 percent on May 20, one week after the shooting. By July 1, his delegate support from primaries had slipped back to roughly 18 percent. Yet, as Figure 1-b shows, rank-and-file poll support for Wallace continued to increase throughout June despite the shooting. He was cutting into the constituency of one of the other candidates. It was unlikely to be McGovern because as Wallace gained, so did McGovern. The answer is clearly revealed in a Gallup poll analysis released just before the New Hampshire primary.[9] We assume once more that the Democratic center consists of Humphrey-Muskie-Jackson; the survey shows that 68 percent supported a center candidate for the nomination while only 7 percent supported McGovern. But with Wallace included in the list of possibilities, support for the center declines by 11 percent whereas McGovern loses only 1 percent.

The Democratic center was badly hurt by the Wallace candidacy. The shift in attention from the insurgency of Wallace to that of McGovern, as a result of the assassination attempt, may have heightened the impression that McGovern was gaining at the expense of support for the center. But the shift in attention did not slow the growth in support for Wallace, and by June 16, the combined support for the two insurgents represented a majority of rank-and-file Democrats, at least in terms of measured support in public opinion polls. By June, the center was in disarray; the preconvention process did not, as Figure 1-b shows, result in a convergence of public support around one candidate. The party was truly divided.

If public opinion among rank-and-file Democrats was divided, so was delegate support. As a comparison of Figures 1-a and 1-b reveals, the percentage growths in delegate strength through the medium of state conventions and the growth of favorable public opinion are roughly equal. Figure 1-a also shows that the moderate surge in delegate support came late in the preconvention period as a result of the California primary. It is somewhat ironic that the effect McGovern's California victory seemed to have had on the remaining state conventions was precisely what J. P. Maloney, the Humphrey strategist, had forecast for Humphrey if he won the primary. Victory in the primaries, Maloney said, would "be the most meaningful influence on delegates chosen in non–primary states." [10] So it was, as Figure 1-a shows.

Of all the factors contributing to McGovern's success—the weakness at the party's center, the Wallace candidacy, the intensity of McGovern's support, the impact of his narrow California victory, and the reform rules—the center's weakness relative to the intensity of support for the McGovern organization seems most important.[11] Of course, it was possible that the intense, well-organized McGovern movement could take advantage of rule changes, but we think that the intensity and organization of the McGovernites, when compared to the Muskie and Humphrey efforts, was far more decisive. This comment leads us back to our original proposition about the effects of the reform rules on the number of amateur delegates at Miami. The relationship between the reform rules and the large number of political amateurs can be summarized as follows: (1) Most of McGovern's success in the nomination struggle is explained by factors other than the new rules on group quotas and procedural openness. (2) The McGovern insurgent candidacy attracted a large number of supporters; some of them became delegates who were issue oriented and politically inexperienced, but many of them would have been delegates at Miami had there been no convention reform. (3) Finally, the group quotas, especially for youth, may have amplified the fundamentally amateur activist nature of the McGovern delegates. Thus, a reasonable evaluation of the effects of the reforms on representation at the 1972 convention must separate these effects from the effects of insurgency. In this chapter, we will attempt to do this for both political experience and the issue opinions of delegates.

Group Representation and Political Experience

Young people, blacks, and women had been severely underrepresented at the 1968 convention. In 1972, the representation of these groups was greatly increased, although blacks were the only group able to reach a percentage equal to their percentage in the population. Table 1 presents the percentage

TABLE 1. Representation of Blacks, Youth, and Women [12]

	1968 convention	1972 convention	Population percentage
Blacks	6%	14%	11%
Under thirty	2	23	30
Women	14	36	51
Total	2,528	3,100	

of each of these groups at the 1968 and 1972 conventions and their approximate percentages in the population.

The changes in representation of these groups also affected that of other groups. Students, for example, who represented only .5 percent of the 1968 convention, comprised over 8 percent of the 1972 convention. Teachers, numerous under Eugene McCarthy in 1968, were a healthy 22 percent of the total delegates at Miami in 1972. As might be expected with increased female representation in 1972, the percentage of housewives rose from 4 percent to 11 percent. But some other occupational groups suffered a decline as a consequence of the new guidelines. Lawyers, for instance, declined from 30 percent in 1968 to 8 percent in 1972, while businessmen dropped from 29 percent to 8 percent in 1972. Perhaps because of the large number of delegates still in school, those holding college degrees declined from 63 percent in 1968 to 55 percent in 1972. Thus, the intended changes in representation of blacks, women, and youth had unintended consequences as well.

But the principal argument concerning the group quotas involves their effects on the number of political amateurs at the convention and on the unrepresentative nature of the opinions of the delegates. The allegation that the number of amateurs increased sharply in 1972 receives some support if one uses as his measure of political experience the number of prior conventions attended by a delegate. But this allegation lacks substance because other measures, such as holding party or public office, underwent little change between 1968 and 1972.[13] Table 2 shows this relationship.

TABLE 2. Comparison of Delegates' Party Experience

	1968 convention	1972 convention	Percentage change
Public office	18%	17%	−1%
Party office	14	15	+1
Attended at least one previous convention	34	16	−18
Total delegates	3,073	3,100	

Changes in levels of political experience from one convention to another seem to be determined, at least in part, by the extent to which the candidate of the party regulars dominates the convention. When an incumbent President, such as Lyndon

B. Johnson in 1964, is being renominated, the number of public and party office holders tends to be high. In fact, in 1964 the percentage of delegates holding public office was twice as high as in 1968. Although Humphrey did not have the direct advantages of incumbency, he was the epitome of the party regular in 1968. So despite the decline from 1964 to 1968, the representation of political experience in 1968 was probably above average.

Before comparing the effects of group quotas and the McGovern insurgency on the levels of political experience represented at the 1972 convention, let us examine the changes in the political experience of the three groups affected by group quotas—blacks, women, and youth. In 1968, men were four times as likely as women to hold public office (20 percent compared to 5 percent), but women were somewhat more likely than men to hold party office or to have attended previous conventions. As one might expect, the 1972 women were much less likely to have attended a previous convention or to be party or public office holders than were the male delegates. In general, women at the 1972 convention were much less experienced than were their counterparts in 1968. If one takes as a measure of political experience the percentage of women with prior convention experience, or party office, or public office, women show the largest decline from 1968 to 1972 of any group. (See Figure 2.)

In 1968, black delegates display a pattern somewhat different from that of women. They were much less likely than whites to have held party office or to have attended a prior convention, and were almost four times less likely to have held a public office. In 1972, as Table 1 shows, there was a sharp increase in the percentage of black delegates but, unlike women, the percentage of "experienced" delegates did not decline dramatically. In fact, the percentage of blacks holding public office rose from 12 percent in 1968 to 19 percent in 1972; for those holding party office it went from 4 percent in 1968 to 10 percent in 1972. Our third measure of political experience—attendance at prior conventions—showed a moderate decline from 19 percent in 1968 to 13 percent in 1972. But the decline for blacks was in no way as severe as the decline from 35 to 16 percent for whites. Using our combined measure of political experience—

holding either public or party office, or having attended a prior convention—the data in Figure 2 for blacks show a 12 percent decline in political experience.

Youth in 1968, like women and blacks, were much less likely than their elders to have held public office. (See Table 1.) But unlike women, they were less likely to have attended a prior convention. The 1972 convention preserved the gap in political experience between young and old because both groups declined equally. (See Figure 2.)

Figure 2 not only traces the decline in political experience

FIGURE 2.

Comparison of Delegate Political Experience: 1968 and 1972

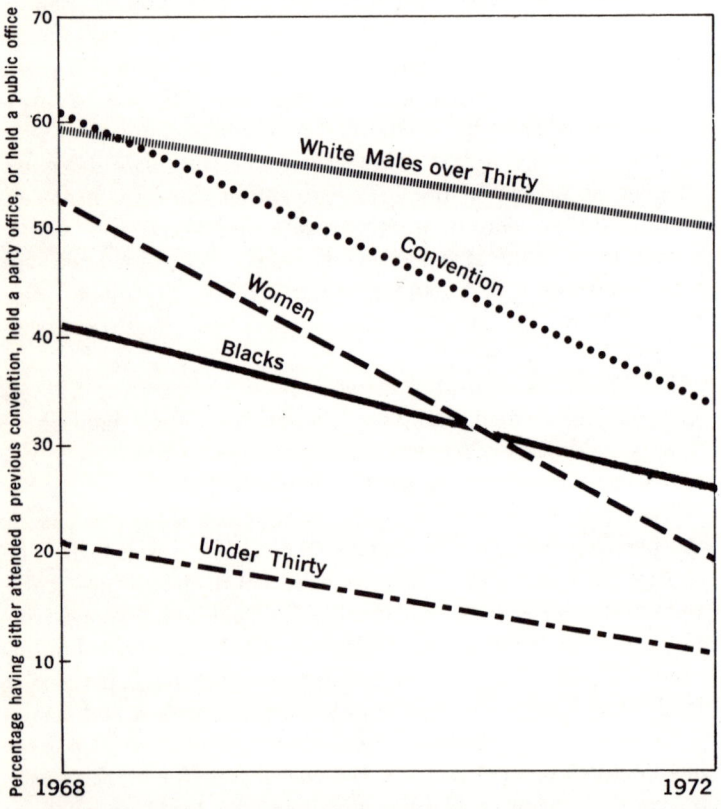

Source: Dartmouth Project IMPRESS convention delegate data files, 1968 and 1972. For a description, see Note 12.

from 1968 for women, blacks, and those under thirty; it shows the sharp decline in political experience for the convention as a whole from 1968 to 1972, from a little over 60 percent in 1968 to a little over 30 percent in 1972. As we have argued throughout this chapter, the decline might be explained by two factors: first, the successful insurgency of both McGovern and Wallace and, second, the group quotas. We can isolate the effects of these two factors by dividing 1968 and 1972 convention delegates according to their support for a regular (Humphrey in 1968 or Humphrey-Muskie-Jackson in 1972) or for an insurgent (McCarthy in 1968 and McGovern-Wallace in 1972). Figure 3-a shows the changes in political experience from 1968 to 1972 for those supporting a regular candidate; Figure 3-b does the same for the insurgent.[14]

In comparing Figure 3-a, which shows the political experience of the regulars in 1968, with Figure 2, showing the same data for the entire convention, it should be noted that the percentages are remarkably close—65 percent for regulars versus 63 percent for the entire convention. The Humphrey organization dominated 1968; the average delegate was a Humphrey supporter with substantial political experience. It should also be noted that the level of political experience among regular supporters of Humphrey dropped approximately 15 percent from 1968 to 1972, while the overall decrease in political experience from 1968 to 1972 was almost twice as large. The extraordinary decline in the number of politically experienced delegates is due in large measure to the success of McGovern, for 1972 was a year in which the typical delegate was an amateur McGovernite. It turns out that approximately half of the decline in political experience can be attributed to the strength of McGovern's candidacy.

Group quotas seem to be responsible for the other half of the decline in political experience. The relevant comparisons are represented in Figures 3-a and 3-b, which show the decline in political experience among regular and insurgent Democrats as a consequence of quotas. In both cases, the drop in the "Regulars" line in Figure 3-a, and the "Insurgents" line in Figure 3-b, is around 15 percent, a decrease from 65 to 50 percent for regulars and from 40 to a little under 30 percent for insurgents. The downward slopes of the two lines are

FIGURE 3.

Comparison of Delegate Political Experience: 1968 and 1972

3a – Regulars*

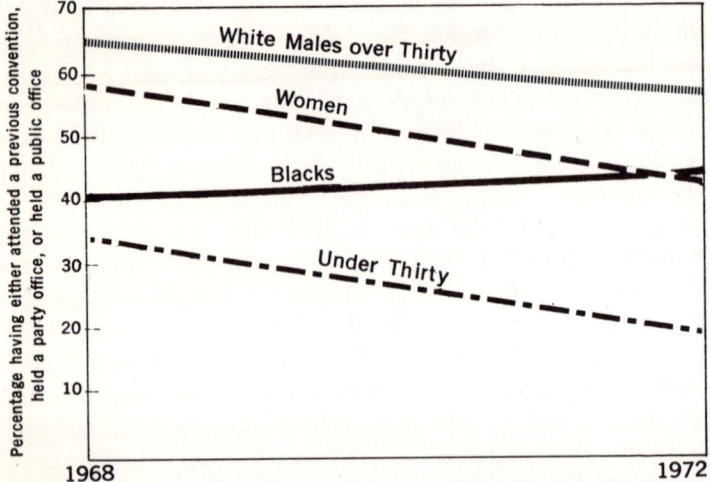

* Regulars supported Humphrey in 1968 and either Muskie or Humphrey in 1972. Both of these categories are by definition and deal with the main thrust of the campaigns involved — not individual delegates.

3b – Insurgents*

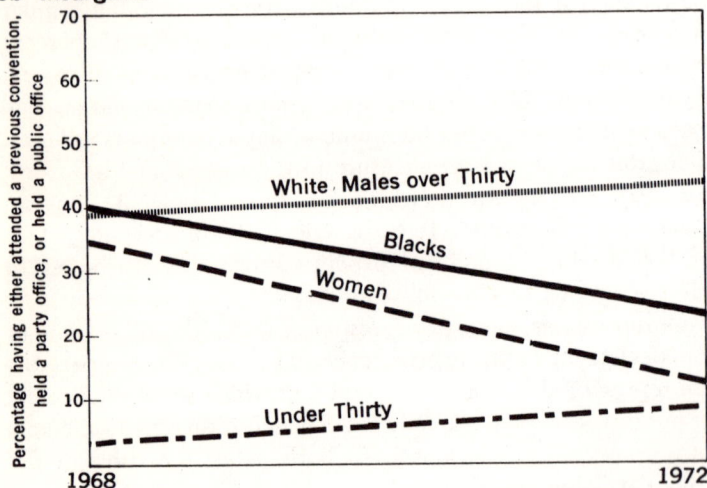

* Insurgents supported McCarthy in 1968 and McGovern in 1972.

Source: Dartmouth Project IMPRESS convention delegate data files, 1968 and 1972. For a description, see Note 12.

almost the same, which means that group quotas have the same effects for both insurgents and regulars. If we assume the McCarthy forces to be typical of insurgent forces in a non-quota convention, then we predict that a convention dominated by a McCarthy or McGovern type of insurgent would diminish the number of delegates with political experience by roughly 15 to 20 percent; and quotas, like those used in 1972 would diminish the number by an additional 15 percent. The size of shifts depends, of course, upon the size of the insurgent effect—the percentage change in the number of insurgents from one convention to another.

The downward slope of the line labeled "Convention" in Figure 2 shows the precise decline in political experience (28 percent) that we want to explain. We have thus far attributed 15 percent of the decline to group quotas, and the remaining 13 percent have been called the insurgency effect. A little less than half of the 15 percent decline due to group quotas turns out to be attributable to the increased representation of youth at the convention. Women account for around 40 percent; the remainder of the decline is accounted for by the increases in black representation. One might have expected results somewhat like these. The young are, almost by definition, inexperienced and disadvantaged in party and public office holding. Yet they make up a substantial segment of the population. The largest gap in political experience (Figures 3-a and 3-b) is between youth and all other groups. Any substantial increase in representation of youth would, of course, have profoundly affected the amount of political experience represented at the convention. In fact, the percentage contributions to the decline in political experience by each of the three groups seems to follow a simple rule involving the relative size of the group in the population, the extent to which it was underrepresented in 1968, and its relative political experience level. Thus, for blacks. who have more political experience than the other two groups and who make up a smaller percentage of the total population, the cost in terms of the loss in political experience is very slight. For women, whose levels of political experience are slightly lower and who make up a larger percentage of the population, the cost in political experience is greater.

As we have tried to show in this section, a valid assessment of the effect of group quotas must separate out the insurgent effect, and it must state the specific groups included in a quota system. By almost any measure we have used, the costs in representing blacks in some reasonable relation to their numbers in the population do not involve much sacrifice in terms of political experience or, as we shall show in the next section, in representativeness of opinion.

Issue Opinions—1972

The reform guidelines for delegate selection have been criticized for turning over the party to elements whose policy views were outside the mainstream. The criticism seems based, in part, on delegate reaction to platform issues that were not part of previous platforms. Perhaps the consideration, or mere mention, of the minority planks on gay liberation and legalization of drugs caused regular party Democrats to feel that the 1972 convention was extremist. But, of course, minority planks are not necessarily representative of the views of the rank-and-file delegates.

A better guide to how extreme the delegates' views were comes from a survey of delegate attitudes toward three important issues: busing to achieve racial balance, amnesty for those who left the country to avoid the draft, and guaranteed annual income. Only one of these issues, a guaranteed annual income, can be considered anywhere near the mainstream of Democratic ideology, but all these issues were important to both delegates and the general public in 1972.

If the Democratic delegates were extremist in their policy opinions, one would expect large discrepancies between delegate opinions and those of the Democratic rank and file.

But before we can directly compare the two groups, it is important to consider the findings of previous research, which have shown that differences in issue opinions have always existed between delegates and the average Democrat in society. Herbert McClosky, in his study of the 1956 Democratic and Republic conventions, found that Democratic delegates were consistently more liberal than the Democratic rank and file, while Republican delegates were more conservative than the average Republican.[15] The difference, McClosky goes on to explain, is a result of the fact that delegates are, in part, samples of political elites. They know more about, and are more interested in, party policy than is the average party member. The differences that McClosky highlighted in 1956 will probably be with us as long as delegates possess these elite characteristics.

In order to assess the impact of the reform rules on the policy opinions of delegates we would need to compare, as we did for the issue of "political experience," the conventions of 1968 and 1972, but the relevant data for such a comparison are not available. We do not even have an appropriate baseline from which to consider the effects of the reform. We can, however, compare the 1972 delegates with rank-and-file party members. According to McClosky, we should find that delegates are slightly more liberal than rank-and-file party members. But if very large differences occur—beyond what the McClosky model predicts—then we would have some evidence for a reform rule effect. In addition, as was the case in our analysis of political experience, we must be able to separate the effects of insurgency from the effects of the quota system.

On the issue of busing, which has divided the party, it is difficult to compare delegates and rank and filers because of variations in question wording. Table 3 does show, however, that a majority of the delegates in 1972 opposed the unqualified use of busing to achieve racial balance and educational equality.[16] The modal delegate response—54 percent of the total—shows a reluctant support of busing if it is the only means for achieving racial balance and educational equality. The relatively small minority of 25 percent that favored busing in an unqualified way was somewhat smaller than its counterpart in the Democratic rank and file. But the evidence for rank-and-file support is based on only two options—favor or oppose. If rank-and-file Democrats had been given the same three options presented to the delegates, the 30 percent might have shrunk considerably, though it is hard to imagine a decline that would bring it down much beyond the 25 percent figure for delegates. Although the data indicate that a small minority of both delegates and rank-and-file Democrats supported busing without any qualification, they also show the rank and file to be far more opposed than delegates to busing in any sense. If we make the rather generous assumption that one-third of the rank-and-file group that is opposed to busing really favors a more qualified option (say, the second option in Table 3), rank and filers would still be far more opposed (47 percent) to busing than would delegates (21 percent).

TABLE 3. Difference Between Delegates and Democratic Rank and File on Issue Opinions

	Delegates	Rank and file
BUSING		
Favor busing with no qualifications	25%	30%
Favor busing if only means to racial balance and educational equality	54	Not available
Oppose	21	70
AMNESTY		
Favor without punishment	46	31
Favor with punishment	36	Not available
Oppose	18	69
GUARANTEED ANNUAL INCOME		
Favor	74	43
Oppose	26	57

Data from Gallup Opinion Indexes, Spring 1972, except for Guaranteed Annual Income. See note 16 for exact wording of questions. "Don't know" and "no" answers were excluded from the tabulations.

The conclusions we have developed for the issue of busing seem to hold for amnesty as well, although the difference between delegates and rank and filers in their support for unqualified amnesty was slightly larger than the corresponding difference for unqualified busing. And if the public sample had been offered the choice of amnesty with punishment, the 36 percent figure might have been further reduced. But in light of the stereotyping of 1972 convention delegates, it is still important to note, as we did for busing, that only a minority of the delegates supported unqualified amnesty. Concerning the extent to which there was unqualified opposition to amnesty, we can again conclude that it was greater among rank and filers than among delegates. Assuming that one-third, at most, of the rank and filers would have endorsed the middle option–

amnesty with punishment—if it had been available, the rank-and-file Democrats are 28 percent more opposed (46 percent) than are the delegates (18 percent).

On the third issue in our analysis, guaranteed annual income, the differences are much larger and clearer. Although the wording of the questions asked of delegates and average Democrats differed, each group was presented with only two options—favor and oppose. The results, presented in Table 3, show a substantial gap between delegates and rank-and-file Democrats. If the alternatives presented to the delegates had been more discriminating ones, however, more revealing differences might have been unearthed.

As with the issue of political experience, it is difficult to attribute the gap between delegates and average Democrats solely, or even in a major sense, to the quota system. Any such analysis would ignore the fact that Democratic convention delegates in past years have been more liberal than Democrats in society at large. There are three basic alternative, or possibly complementary, explanations: (1) the normal distance between the liberalism of Democratic elites and followers, (2) the group quotas, and (3) the short-term insurgency effect of McGovern's victory in the preconvention period.

Considering the first quota group—youth—younger delegates tended to be much more liberal than older delegates on all three issues, and the same generation gap can be found within the rank and file. But, without question, the cleavage between young and old delegates is far greater than it is between young and old rank and filers. A good portion of this generation gap is due to the younger delegates being far more liberal than young rank and filers. This was not so much a result of youth quotas as it was of the attractiveness of McGovern for the young issue-oriented, college-educated activists. The Humphrey–Muskie young delegates were not far removed from their rank-and-file counterparts. It seems that the short-term forces favoring McGovern, rather than the quotas, produced young delegates with such liberal opinions on the issues.

For women, it would be hard to argue that the group quotas somehow produced a convention more liberal than would be expected as a result of Democratic leaders being more liberal than Democratic followers. The distance between women delegates and rank-and-file women is about as great as that between male delegates and male rank and filers, but women in general were more liberal than men on each of the issues. The increase in the representation of women, then, tended to make the convention as a whole a bit more liberal simply because rank-and-file women are more liberal than rank-and-file men.

A comparison of delegate issue opinions of blacks with those of whites reveals very large differences. Black delegates are far more liberal than white delegates on each of the three issues. But unlike youth and, to a lesser extent, women, the opinions of black delegates on busing, guaranteed annual income, and amnesty are close to those of black rank-and-file Democrats. The increased number of black delegates in 1972 surely liberalized the convention by bringing it closer to the views of the party's black constituency.

Out of our examination of black, female, and youth issue orientations, a pattern emerges that sheds some light on what appears to be an extraordinarily liberal Democratic convention. In 1972, the three determinants of the liberalism gap between Democratic leaders and followers—the McClosky mass-elite model, the group quotas, and the McGovern insurgency—reinforced each other. Possibly, this may always happen in insurgency years. In past noninsurgent conventions, however, the factors have tended to work against each other and thus shorten the distance between leaders and followers: the underrepresentation of the more liberal groups formed by women, blacks, and youth (and it must be remembered that these groups are not vastly more liberal) tended to counterbalance the natural tendency of the Democratic elite to be more liberal than its followers. In 1972, because the candidates of the Democratic center did not effectively mobilize their forces, the McGovern insurgency added greatly to the liberalism gap. Given this pattern, then, it would be sheer folly to argue that somehow the reform rules adopted for the 1972 convention directly resulted in an unrepresentative convention.

Conclusion: Goals and Consequences of Representation

Proponents of increased group representation have cited two major goals. First, if a group's numerical strength at a conven-

The Impact of Reform on Representation

tion is increased, then the members of that group in the society at large will be inclined to accord more legitimacy to the convention's decisions. For example, quite apart from the delegates' stands on issues, blacks may feel that a convention's decisions are more legitimate if a sizeable number of blacks has participated in the decision making. A second goal of representation is directly related to issues. Proponents have argued that greater numbers of blacks, women, and youth would permit group members to articulate and define group interests more effectively.

But to the extent that increased group representation does result in diminishing the number of party professionals, it runs against the grain of yet another theory of representation.[17] In this theory, it is not so important that the convention have the same issue opinions as the party's constituency, nor is it vital that the proportion of blacks, women, or the young be the same in the convention as in the party constituency. What is vital, however, is the capacity of the convention to take into account, in its choice of candidate and platform, the views and interests of its constituency. It may well be that political experience, or a sense of professionalism, is what must be represented in large amounts at a convention. Thus, one might argue that the 15 percent reduction in political experience as a consequence of quotas is too high a price to pay. But we can only measure the exchange if we can come to understand the increase in legitimacy engendered among the various constituencies who gained and, conversely, the loss in legitimacy among groups who felt deprived by the quota system. It is clear, as we have pointed out, that in terms of representation of issue opinions of a constituency, and in terms of political experience, the increase in representation of blacks in 1972 was least costly and, in fact, represented an adjustment to the political reality of the party's dependence on black support.

To comprehend fully why some party leaders have advanced the proposition that the so-called quota system was responsible for the radicalization of the convention, one must understand that such an assertion has political functions; that believing it to be true may affect the distribution of power within the party. Its political functions seem to have been (1) to discredit spokesmen for the new constituencies as being radical and, as a consequence, without broad support, and (2) to signal the old constituencies in the party-labor, blue-collar factions, and so forth, that they are returning to positions of leadership within the party. Thus, for some, it becomes convenient to attribute a variety of the party's current ailments to the quota system.

The group quota reform was written, in part, to express a perceived change in the distribution of power. Had McGovern won in November, praise would have been heaped on the quota system for broadening the constituent base of the party to include new groups. But the new groups did not provide the margin of victory. Thus, for critics of the group quotas, the party's electoral disaster in November 1972 raised anew the question of how much power the new groups actually wielded.[18] Yet, changing the rules in the wake of defeat posed other problems for the party.

The original reforms, and even the more recent demands for their modification, are expressed in ways that make it difficult to take into account important group differences.[19] The new groups differ in size, cohesiveness, and past contribution to party success. Those who espoused the reforms saw these group differences as fundamentally irrelevant; those who wish to abolish the national party quota provision feel that a relatively free and open political process will take relevant group differences into account.[20]

The very universality of the quota rule—as it applies to underrepresented groups—prevents modifications that would reflect group differences. Yet, if scrapping the quotas would result in a reduction of group representation back to the 1968 levels, it might well be a political disaster for the party. For example, the reduction in black representation might be seen as a racist move by this important voting group.[21] However, if the party adopted rules maintaining quotas for blacks, but not for women or youth, it would amount to a denial of the argument forming the intellectual basis for the criticism of the reform rules. For the party regulars, a solution was needed that would be consistent with the argument for eliminating the quotas and that would reflect, at the same time, the relative power positions of the affected groups. A rule change that met both constraints would, first, decentralize the establishment of quotas by eliminating the national party provisions, and, second, increase the role of state and local party elites in the delegate slate-making process. Slate making, or group quotas based on important constituency elements, would then be more under the control of state and local party leaders.[22]

Clearly, the adoption of the above plan would constitute a partial return to a more traditional system. However, the raised expectations among blacks, women, and youth in the 1972 experiment could not prudently be ignored by traditional party leaders. Although guesses about the precise form that minority group representation might take in the future are risky, our analysis does suggest a direction. Ranking the groups affected by the 1972 quota provisions in terms of a composite measure of relative size, group cohesiveness, and contribution to party success, the order would surely be (1) blacks, (2) women, and (3) youth. If the party adopts something like the above plan and does abolish the group quotas, youth should suffer the sharpest decline in representation, followed by women, and then by blacks.

In politics, very little is what it seems to be at first glance. Conservative Democrats say the quota system must be abolished; yet they want quotas for senior party leaders.[23] The issue, we think, has never been the presence or absence of quotas; rather, it has been which groups should receive their protection, how decentralized the system should be, and, finally, how formally the requirement should be stated. Parties are not dissimilar from other organizations in their concern for quotas. Private universities acknowledge, for example, the financial support of alumni through quotas for their offspring. In a broader sense, then, many organizations develop ways of recognizing, as well as appealing to, important segments of the organization's environment through quotas or their functional equivalents.

NOTES

1. The quotations are taken from our interviews with delegates.

2. For example, the somewhat conservative Coalition for a Democratic Majority Task Force has published in draft form *Towards*

Fairness and Unity for '76, its proposals for modifying the reform rules, based on the assumption that party defeat was "due to the public impression . . . that the . . . convention which nominated [McGovern] did not represent the mainstream of Democratic ideas, values, and political leadership" (p. 4). The report goes on to attribute the unrepresentative nature of the convention to the reform rules on delegate selection.

3. The precise wording, which need not be repeated here, is contained in the official report of the reform commission, *Mandate for Reform*.

4. *Congressional Quarterly*, April 17, 1973, p. 847.

5. Most standard histories are full of such accounts. See, for example, Gerold Pomper, *Nominating the President* (Chicago: Northwestern University Press, 1963).

6. What may have helped McGovern, in the end, was the simple fact that a larger percentage of the delegates were selected through primaries—63 percent in 1972 compared with 42 percent in 1968.

7. Winning California in June and using the victory to promote support in the remaining state conventions was a strategy followed by Goldwater in 1964, as well as Humphrey and McGovern in 1972.

8. James W. Davis, *Presidential Primaries: Road to the White House* (New York: Thomas Y. Crowell, 1967), p. 94.

9. *Congressional Quarterly*, March 25, 1972, p. 657.

10. *National Journal*, vol. 4, no. 27 (July 1, 1972): 1086.

11. Politicians tend to simplify arguments that favor their power positions. Thus, conservative Democrats drop all factors from the list except the reform rules.

12. Data are primarily a collation of information gathered in the preconvention period in a CBS News telephone poll and in questionnaires mailed to the delegates by Newsweek magazine and the Ripon Society. All data were analyzed with the IMPRESS system at Dartmouth.

13. The data on public office holding may deceive the unwary reader. Had we drawn the line between holding a national public office or not, the 1968–1972 comparison would have revealed a sharp drop in the percentage of national public office holders.

14. Of course, the comparison assumes McCarthy and McGovern to be typical insurgents from the Democratic Left and, thus, reasonably representative samples from the population of insurgent activists. But even if that assumption is granted, we still have a sampling problem because of the small number of McCarthyites at the 1968 convention.

15. Herbert McClosky et al., "Issue Conflict and Consensus Among Party Leaders and Followers," *American Political Science Review*, vol. 54 (June 1960): 406–27.

16. The questions asked of delegates were:
   1) Which of the following statements comes closest to your own position on the issue of busing school children?
   —I am wholeheartedly in favor of busing to achieve integration and equal education. (22 percent)
   —I don't like busing but I support it when it is the only available tool to achieve integration and equal education. (47 percent)
   —I oppose busing as a means to achieve integration and equal education. (18 percent)
   —no answer. (13 percent)

   2) What about the question of amnesty for Americans who left the country to avoid military service during the Vietnam war? Would you say that you:
   —favor immediate amnesty without any conditions attached. (21 percent)
   —favor amnesty without conditions, but after all our troops have been withdrawn and prisoners released. (19 percent)
   —favor amnesty but with the condition that those involved perform some sort of national service. (31 percent)
   —oppose amnesty of any kind. (16 percent)
   —no answer. (13 percent)

   3) There have been various proposals calling for some sort of guaranteed annual income for all people. Without getting into the specifics of each plan, generally speaking, do you:
   —favor the idea of guaranteed annual income. (64 percent)
   —oppose the idea of guaranteed annual income. (23 percent)
   —no answer. (13 percent)

The Gallup organization asked the following question on busing between August 27 and 30, 1971: "In general, do you favor or oppose the busing of Negro and white school children from one school district to another?"

For guaranteed annual income, Gallup asked in January of 1969; "As you may know, there is talk about giving every family an income of at least $3,200 a year, which would be the amount for a family of four. If the family earns less than this, the government would make up the difference. Would you favor or oppose such a plan?" This question mentions a specific plan; the question asked of the delegates does not.

On amnesty, Gallup asked the following question between June 23 and 26, 1972: "Do you think young men who have left the United States to avoid the draft (A) SHOULD be allowed to return to this country without some form of punishment, or (B) SHOULD NOT be allowed to return to this country without some form of punishment?"

17. *Towards Fairness,* op. cit., p. 4. The party regular arguments below are taken from this document.

18. Ibid., p. 25. ". . . fashionable to argue that potent new forces out of which a new political coalition would emerge; the minorities, the women. . . . The 1972 election provided a clear test of this new political outlook."

19. Ibid., p. 2. "We believe underrepresented groups win real victories only when they have organized themselves to win elections." This seems to deny (1) racism as a basis for underrepresentation, and (2) that real political groups may be invigorated by quotas.

20. Ibid.

21. Ibid., p. 5. The report expressed concern about this, but shrugged it off with an "equal opportunity of participation" clause.

22. Ibid., p. 14. The report recommends that 20 percent of a state's delegation be chosen by state party committees.

23. Ibid., pp. 13–14.

chapter three

Arenas of Decision
Innovation in Group Representation at the Convention

At a national nominating convention, delegates may make decisions about a number of things: the choice of a nominee for President, the resolution of credentials disputes, the writing of platform planks, the adoption of party rules, and the choice of a nominee for Vice-President. The media and scholarly books tell us of bargaining between candidates and groups of delegates, but where does such bargaining take place? Where does the real work of the convention take place? Where are decisions made that affect the important outcomes of a convention? This essay will focus on the arenas of decision—the sites where delegates meet to persuade each other, to bargain with each other, and to make up their minds about which courses of action to follow.

Students of past conventions have observed that many delegates do not become involved to any great extent in the work of the convention. Rather, they see themselves as spectators or as detached students of the convention proceedings. Or they regard the convention as a vacation site and devote themselves mainly to recreational pursuits.[1]

According to the classic model of convention decision making, the key units for bargaining are the state delegations. This model assumes that such delegations, operating under the unit rule, bargain with each other and with candidate organizations. The rank-and-file delegates are manipulated by hierarchical leaders holding leading roles in national, state, or local party organizations.[2]

The 1972 Democratic convention was marked by a number of changes in the convention rules and in the nature of the delegates that appeared to falsify some basic assumptions of the classic model. The reform commission of the national Democratic party had laid down a set of requirements for the state parties to follow in order to open the delegate selection process to wider participation. State parties were required to publish specific rules for the delegate selection process: all delegates had to be elected either in primaries or in state conventions; public notice had to be given for all meetings connected with the process; state parties had to wait until 1972 before initiating the delegate selection procedure; and the use of the unit rule [3] was abolished. It could be expected that these changes would make it harder for a party leader or high elected official to control the votes of a state delegation. Thus, the importance of hierarchical state-delegation leaders in the bargaining process would be reduced. Dissident forces within the delegation could be sought out by candidate organizations or other state leaders who were attempting to fashion winning coalitions. With decision-making power at the convention more widely dispersed, there would be an increase in the number of groups to be consulted in forming coalitions and this would strain an already burdened information system. Thus, there would be strong incentives to find ways to assemble the smaller groups into more manageable bargaining units.

The expected desire, and need, to develop new kinds of bargaining units appeared to coincide with new forms of group representation at the convention. With the increase in participation by women, youths, blacks, and nonparty activists of all kinds, state delegations would be subject to even more factionalization than might be predicted by the change in the unit rule. It became clear that interest-group representation at the convention would go beyond the traditional testimony on the platform and the holding of labor-union receptions. In the spring of 1972 there were calls for black caucuses, women's caucuses, youth caucuses—the formation of new arenas for bargaining. With strong loyalties to their race, sex, or age group, the participants in such new caucuses might be expected to take these meetings very seriously.

Thus, it appeared that in 1972, convention decision making might conform to a somewhat different model. According to this model, the importance of state delegations as arenas of decision would be decreased, and the need for new bargaining units would be met by the emergence of group caucuses of blacks, women, and youth. The activists who advocated strong group caucuses were voicing a recurring theme of the protest movements of the 1960s—that the interests of disadvantaged groups could only be represented by members of those groups. Critics of the Democratic party's past treatment of such groups argued that white, middle-aged males could not be trusted to protect the interests of less advantaged groups. Therefore, blacks at the convention should unite to speak for the interests of black people, women should speak for women, and so on.

Before the convention began, both journalists and political activists expected the group caucuses to be important arenas of decision.[4] This essay will examine the experiences of the caucuses, analyze the organizational problems they faced, and discuss perceptions of the caucuses, both on the part of their participants and on the part of the other delegates.

The Convention Examined: Recreation Versus Work

As we have noted, some delegates at past conventions regarded the convention site as a vacation ground. Such delegates would not be searching for an arena of decision making in state delegation, group caucus, or anywhere else. But interviews with the 1972 delegates revealed that the vast majority were devoting themselves strenuously to convention-related business. This was not surprising, in view of the fact that three of the convention sessions lasted until well past 3:00 A.M. Marathon sessions, combined with state delegation meetings, were a heavy drain on the delegates' time. If, in addition, a delegate wished to attend other caucuses or work for a candidate, there was barely enough time left to eat and sleep. We asked delegates how they were spending their time in Miami. Some of the responses were:

"Sleeping and on the convention floor and caucuses. Strictly with the work of the convention."

"Are you kidding? I haven't been to bed. I haven't seen a thing."

"No recreation. I take it very seriously."

"Either in caucuses or at the convention—*all of my time*. Lots of state delegation caucuses."

"Working for Wallace. We keep in close touch with his people."

"Lobbying until the last minute."

Focus on Arenas

Having discovered that the delegates described themselves as working hard on convention-related business, let us now examine some of the sites where convention activity was carried on. A wide variety of new special caucuses were in evidence; among them, the Black Caucus, Women's Caucus, Youth Caucus, Latin Caucus, Senior Citizens' Caucus, and Jewish Caucus, as well as the state delegations. We will briefly describe the experiences of the various special caucuses, and identify some of the recurring organizational problems with which they had to contend. These problems, which were not widely foreseen before the convention, constituted serious obstacles to the achievement of stated organizational ends, and they made it harder for the special caucuses to compete successfully with state delegations for the time and attention of delegates.

THE BLACK CAUCUS.[5] Long before the opening of the convention, black delegates had been making plans to meet with each other in Miami Beach. A National Black Political Convention had been held in Gary, Indiana, on March 1 through 12, 1972, which drew up an agenda of issues and demands relating to blacks. And the Congressional Black Caucus had promulgated its own, somewhat milder, Black Bill of Rights. Calls for black unity, and the assertion of black interests, were common. Shirley Chisholm's candidacy disturbed some black leaders, because she made a unilateral decision to run and did not wait for endorsement by a unified black caucus. Another crack in black unity came when a group of Congressional Black Caucus members—Representatives Louis Stokes, Walter Fauntroy, and William Clay—decided to support Senator McGovern. Black supporters of other candidates complained that black solidarity had been violated. Although these disagreements caused considerable bitterness, many black leaders continued to hope that a unified black caucus at the convention would agree on a common set of issue stands and bargain with candidates to secure support for those stands.

Our interviews showed that, at the outset of the convention (Sunday, July 9 and Monday, July 10), black and white delegates had similar expectations concerning the importance of the Black Caucus. (See Table 1.) Of those interviewed, 30

TABLE 1. Percentages of Black and White Delegates Who Believed Black Caucus to Be Most Important Arena *

	Blacks	Whites
Sunday–Monday	30%	28%
	(3)	(21)
Tuesday–Wednesday	67%	15%
	(4)	(9)
Thursday–Friday	60%	5%
	(6)	(2)

* Number of cases upon which percentage is based is included in parentheses. Chi-square probability for blacks is .262; for whites, .012.

percent of the blacks and about 28 percent of the whites viewed the Black Caucus as the site of the most important convention decisions.[6]

On Sunday, July 9, the day before the Democratic National Convention opened, a Black Caucus meeting was scheduled for 2:00 P.M. This meeting was held under the auspices of the Minorities Division of the Democratic National Committee. (A member of the staff of the Minorities Division noted, however, that if the national committee had not scheduled the meeting, the Congressional Black Caucus would have scheduled one of its own.) The meeting was supposed to be open only to black delegates and alternates, and, for a short period while Presidential candidates were addressing the caucus, the press was to be allowed in. Almost immediately, however, the caucus ran into organizational problems. The original plan had called for each delegate and alternate to have his or her name checked off a list before receiving a pass to enter the meeting, but too many people arrived at once for the plan to be workable. And to complicate matters, the list of black delegates and alternates was incomplete. Those who were not listed became angry at being denied entrance to the meeting, and a fight almost started at the door. Eventually, the meeting was declared open to all black people; security guards tried to screen out the media.

The main item of business at the meeting was hearing appeals from the Presidential candidates. Senator Muskie, the first to speak to the caucus, talked about his past accomplishments in the field of domestic legislation. He received a polite response. Shirley Chisholm, who followed Muskie, received a standing ovation when she entered. The enthusiasm for Chisholm was evident throughout the crowd, and she spoke forcefully in behalf of her candidacy. Her frequent use of black "street language" was a solid hit with the audience and helped to put the other candidates at a disadvantage. She cautioned the delegates not to sell their votes, and she made some pointed references to politicians who she claimed had received money for endorsing certain candidates. Her speech ended with a plea to delegates to vote for her on the first ballot. If they were unable to do that, she asked them to vote uncommitted in an effort to show their strength and to gain some bargaining power.

Chisholm's act was a difficult one to follow. Terry Sanford tried to talk about his record on civil rights, but few delegates seemed to be listening. Senator McGovern appeared on the stage with Coretta King and Yancey Martin, a key black aide. The front runner talked about the war and about his grassroots campaign, in an attempt to disassociate himself from the establishment politicians. He discussed the California challenge, which he said involved issues other than that of which candidate a delegate happened to support. And McGovern promised the Black Caucus that, if he won the election, he would place blacks in all levels of government. The response to McGovern was restrained; even McGovern's black delegates did not want to appear disloyal to Chisholm in spirit.

Hubert Humphrey was cheered when he appeared but was booed when he spoke of the evils of winner-take-all primaries. Although he received applause for his discussion of his civil-rights record, he was booed again when he said that he did not make any deals. (Humphrey's statement was apparently designed to justfy his unwillingness to support a list of Black Caucus demands, and the audience was accordingly displeased.)

After the candidates had spoken, the press was cleared from the room, and the meeting went into executive session. The issue of supporting Ralph Abernathy and the National Welfare Rights Organization in their quest for convention seats was the first to be considered. After some discussion, the Black Caucus voted to place one representative from each of the state delegations on the committee negotiating with the NWRO on the convention-seats issue. The matter was not raised again in the Black Caucus.

California Assemblyman Willie Brown, co-chairman of his state delegation, then asked if he could address the caucus from the podium. In his speech, Brown likened the fight by the McGovern people for regaining the full California delegation to challenges made by black people in 1964 and 1968. He stated that his delegation had the best minority representation of any at the convention and that the challenge against the delegation was a challenge against black people. Brown stated that he was the first black man to be a chairman of a state delegation and that the opponents of McGovern's delegation were trying to silence him personally on the convention floor. He tried to disassociate the challenge from the support of any particular candidate and based his appeal on the fact that the caucus should support him as a black man, and his delegation, because of the number of blacks in it. He closed with an emotional appeal: "Brothers and sisters, I'm crying, I'm begging, I'm pleading, I want my delegation." He received a standing ovation.

Brown's use of flamboyant rhetoric was not an unusual occurrence at the Black Caucus; the audience appreciated and applauded dramatic oratory. As a black observer at the caucus said of Brown's speech: "The speech [Brown] gave to the convention was later capsulized, cleaned up, toned down, and given to the convention. What he said to the Black Caucus would only be acceptable to an all-black audience. Brown used the pseudo street-language and intonations that are popular with blacks and give the impression that one is close to 'the people.'"

A speaker against Brown's motion to support his position on the California credentials complained that black people were unhappy at the way they were being treated by McGovern forces in their home states. The speaker stated that blacks could hold the power to give McGovern the nomination on the first ballot or to make it an "open convention." Other delegates rose to express their support of Chisholm and to encourage others to vote for her on the first ballot as a show of strength. One questioner asked Willie Brown whether he could deliver 51 black votes for Chisholm. When Brown replied that California law bound delegates to vote for McGovern, another member of the audience stated that courts had ruled that state law was not binding at the convention. At this point, Mayor Charles Evers asked that delegates request candidates to release black delegates to vote for Chisholm. The meeting was adjourned.

The second meeting of the Black Caucus was held at 10:00 A.M. on Monday, July 10. This meeting started an hour late with only 150 or 200 people present, far fewer than had attended the first meeting. At the start of the meeting, Mayor Richard Hatcher asked people to work together; he suggested that a steering committee composed of one representative from each state be elected in order to further organizational coherence. This suggestion was approved. The caucus then elected Mayor Hatcher to be permanent chairman. (Representative Charles Diggs had been the temporary chairman.)

Charles Evers, reporting on the outcome of his suggestion for candidates to release their black delegates, told the caucus that only Humphrey had agreed to the request. A man then gave a fiery speech supporting Humphrey's release of his delegates, and Imamu Baraka (formerly, Leroi Jones) condemned people who had suddenly "jumped on the Shirley Chisholm bandwagon." He said that such people were devious, did not support Chisholm originally, and were really working for Humphrey or Muskie. In an atmosphere of confusion, the caucus was adjourned until 4:00 P.M.

At the reassembled meeting, the Black Caucus voted to support the Willie Brown–McGovern position on the California challenge and the Jesse Jackson position (against Mayor Daley) on the Illinois challenge. A sheet was to be distributed to black delegates with instructions on how to vote.

At the fourth meeting of the Black Caucus, held on Tuesday, July 11, at 1:00 P.M., the participants tried to determine a way to ensure that only delegates and alternates voted at their meetings, since most of those who were attending were nondelegates. When the meeting began, there were only fifteen delegates and alternates present out of a total group of a hundred. The caucus finally decided that all black people were welcome to the meetings and entitled to vote. It had proved impossible to screen delegates from nondelegates at the entrance; and, after all, it was the nondelegates who were showing most of the interest in the Black Caucus.

In discussing the platform, the Black Caucus went on record as opposing any reports, recommendations, or resolutions that were supported by George Wallace. Before the meeting was adjourned, it was decided to give the Steering Committee the authority to determine the position of McGovern toward black people and to discover what deals or commitments, if any, he had made with black people. The Steering Committee was also charged with finding out if it was still possible for the Black Caucus to negotiate with the candidates.

The final business of the meeting was a report by the Communications Committee on a system it had devised for use at the convention hall. (There had been numerous complaints of disunity and confusion among black delegates on the floor.) The proposed system consisted of a command post in the back of the hall where black delegates could deliver messages to be distributed to each other. The messages would be taken to either Hatcher or Diggs for approval and screening and then would be distributed. It was agreed that all official notices from the Black Caucus would have Hatcher's signature to guarantee authenticity.

On Wednesday, the fifth and final meeting of the Black

Caucus was held. At the outset, Hatcher told the caucus that the purpose of the meeting was to hear reports from representatives of candidates still in the race. The purpose of the reports would be to tell what commitments had been made by each of the candidates to black people. A representative of Shirley Chisholm, speaking first, said that the black Congresswoman wanted to operate a brokerage on behalf of black people—but to do so, she needed their support. Then Walter Fauntroy, representing George McGovern, told the caucus of McGovern's commitment to the National Black Political Agenda (formulated at the Gary meeting) and the Black Bill of Rights (from the Congressional Black Caucus). He said that McGovern had agreed to channel some of the money spent in his campaign through the black community to be used for black voter registration and general campaigning.

Humor, as well as rhetorical flourish, was appreciated by the audience at the Black Caucus. Following Fauntroy's speech, Dick Gregory gave a ten-minute performance as a "representative of George Wallace." (Gregory had provided comic relief earlier in this same role; he told the caucus that Wallace had really given America a message, and that the message was "there is still one white fool in America." Gregory continued: "Y'all know that George is really not sincere on his stand on school busing. Remember, when he opposed integration of the University of Alabama, he stood in front of the door. I haven't seen him stand in front of a bus yet." Laughter erupted from the audience.)

The caucus finally voted, amid turbulent argument, to go on record as supporting the candidacy of Shirley Chisholm, although there was a widespread lack of belief in the significance of this vote for individuals in their eventual decisions on candidates. As delegates were filing out, the caucus also voted to support Imamu Baraka's proposal to give three Black Caucus co-chairmen—along with the Steering Committee—authority to meet with Presidential candidates and to press the demands of black people. The last meeting of the Black Caucus ended.

During the course of the convention, an interesting development occurred in the delegates' perceptions of the Black

Caucus. Although black and white delegates had similar expectations at the outset of the convention about the importance of the caucus, our interview results show that the perceptions of the two groups differed widely at the convention's end. On Thursday and Friday, 60 percent of the black delegates, but only 5.4 percent of the white delegates, saw the Black Caucus as a site for the most important convention decisions. (See Table 1.) It was as if black and white delegates were experiencing two different conventions.

The divergence of perceptions between blacks and whites was clearly evident at the meeting of the Democratic National Committee in Miami Beach on the day after the convention. Senator McGovern nominated Pierre Salinger for vice-chairman of the committee, but black leaders put forward the name of Basil Paterson of New York, a black national committeeman, instead. Senator McGovern, stunned, went to the microphone and told the committee, "Either one of these very able men would be perfectly acceptable to me and a great credit to our party." Then Mr. Salinger, seeking to avoid embarrassment to Senator McGovern, moved to the platform and declared, "I think I sense the feeling in this committee and I would like to withdraw my name."[7] Black leaders complained that the McGovern people did not consult with the Black Caucus before making their nomination, while McGovern staff members appeared to be shocked by the blacks' move. The divergence between white and black perceptions of the Black Caucus' importance appeared wide indeed.

THE WOMEN'S CAUCUS. Women's Caucus activities at the convention were led by, and grew out of, the National Women's Political Caucus, a year-old organization of activists concerned with issues relating to women. Over the weekend before the convention, the NWPC met with more than a hundred delegates and tried to hammer out a set of priorities to fight for on the convention floor. (NWPC, formed in Washington in July of 1971 to "awaken, organize and assert the vast political power represented by women," had called an open meeting for all women delegates for Monday, July 10.)

Leaders of the NWPC urged delegates to concentrate on a number of key issues: the seating of more women in the

South Carolina delegation, which was an important credentials dispute; the unseating of Mayor Daley's delegation, which had few women; and the passing of a platform plank for liberalized abortion laws. In talks before the beginning of the convention, the caucus leaders also discussed the possibility of nominating a woman for the Vice-Presidency. It was hoped that the greatly increased percentage of women delegates (almost 40 percent, compared to 13 percent in 1968) could be translated into greater political power.[8]

Although the hopes of the Women's Caucus leaders were high, only a small number of delegates expected at the beginning of the convention that the caucus would be a site of the most important convention decisions. Expectations did differ by sex, however; women were almost twice as likely as men to expect the caucus to be an important convention site. (See Table 2.)

TABLE 2. Percentages of Women and Men Who Believed Women's Caucus to Be Most Important Arena *

	Women	Men
Sunday–Monday	26% (10)	15% (8)
Tuesday–Wednesday	21% (5)	13% (6)
Thursday–Friday	21% (4)	11% (4)

* Number of cases upon which percentage is based is included in parentheses.

About seven hundred women attended the Women's Caucus meeting on Monday. When former White House aide Liz Carpenter introduced Senator McGovern (one of a number of candidates to address the meeting) she said that McGovern's reforms had been crucial in increasing women's representation. "We know we wouldn't be here if it hadn't been for you," she remarked. McGovern proceeded to get himself into an embarrassing situation when he said that he "really couldn't take credit" for all the women being there. That credit, he remarked, "would have to go to Adam." Boos and hisses followed this remark. McGovern asked: "Can I recover if I say Adam—and Eve?" There was not much response. McGovern saved his position only by promising his "full support" to the South Carolina challenge to seat women. He got cheers for that. Then McGovern asked for women's support on the California challenge and angered some of the women by arguing for "some kind of compromise" on Illinois. A number of those attending the caucus expressed disappointment in McGovern's failure to mention other issues, such as abortion, in which women were specifically interested.[9]

Shirley Chisholm was greeted by a sustained ovation, which lasted about three minutes. She argued against McGovern's California position on the grounds that people voting for other candidates should be represented. Terry Sanford announced that he thought abortion should be a woman's choice. Hubert Humphrey declared that "Racism and sexism is [sic] synonymous." He said, "I've had my difficulties with the male chauvinist press" and pledged his "public life to ending discrimination against women."[10] If he were President, Humphrey promised, there would be women everywhere—in the National Security Council, the cabinet, the Supreme Court, the major committees.

The rally was supposed to have been a time for informing women delegates about how to push for women's issues on the convention floor, but this never occurred. After the candidates left, the crowd dwindled sharply.

Members of the National Women's Political Caucus fought hard to win the votes they had identified as most important for women. The South Carolina challenge, which would have added nine women and subtracted nine men from the delegation, was defeated by a vote of 1,555 to 1,429. But the vote would have been much closer—and the women might even have triumphed—if the McGovern leadership had not shaved votes from their total in order to avoid a parliamentary trap.[11] In this instance, as in a number of others, caucus interests were in opposition to candidate interests. On the second key credentials test identified by the Women's Political Caucus, denying Mayor Daley's delegation its seats and admitting a delegation that had more women and blacks, the women's position was victorious.

The third crucial test was the fight over the minority platform plank on abortion. Actually, the word "abortion" did not appear anywhere in the proposed amendment to the 15-point "rights of women" plank adopted by the convention. The amendment stated that, "In matters relating to human reproduction, each person's right to privacy, freedom of choice, and individual conscience should be fully respected, consistent with relevant Supreme Court decisions." Again, the Women's Caucus clashed with the McGovern organization as the women's activists lobbied for the plank and McGovern aides lobbied against it. The plank was finally defeated, 1,572.80 to 1,101.37. In the final convention decision of interest to the Women's Caucus, the nomination of the Texas State Representative, Frances ("Sissy") Farenthold for Vice-President, the caucus and its male supporters were able to achieve a second-place finish, accumulating over 400 votes for their candidate.

In contrast to the case of the Black Caucus, delegate perceptions of the importance of the Women's Caucus did not undergo large shifts during the week of the convention. According to our interviews, both men and women became slightly less likely to view the Women's Caucus as an important arena of decision. (See Table 2.)

THE YOUTH CAUCUS. On Monday morning, July 10, a meeting of young McGovern delegates was arranged to prepare for that afternoon's meeting of the Youth Caucus. Because of poor notification and bad transportation, however, only about two hundred delegates arrived. (The National Youth Caucus, an organization of liberal youth delegates that ceased to exist before the convention, estimated, before its dissolution, that there were 618 young delegates, 420 of whom were pledged to McGovern. An additional 70 were committed, though not pledged, to the Senator; 70 more were pledged to others but were McGovern sympathizers.)

At the McGovern youth meeting, McGovern staff member Tim Boggs talked about the agenda of the Youth Caucus, a meeting of young delegates to be sponsored by the Democratic National Committee. Supporters of the various candidates had agreed on a caucus chairman—Joe Farmer of

Nebraska. Farmer, an officer of the national Young Democrats, was a nondelegate and was thought to be fair. Boggs explained that, in the caucus itself, there would be a ban on Presidential endorsements. Then McGovern staff member Eli Segal came in to discuss the importance of the California challenge and the parliamentary maneuvering that would lead up to it. Segal explained that, on the South Carolina challenge, the McGovern organization wanted to avoid the parliamentary trap of a vote total that was somewhere between a majority of those voting and an absolute majority of convention delegates. But he stopped short of saying that some votes might have to be shaved to avoid the trap.

Some seven hundred participants had been expected at the afternoon Youth Caucus; youthful door-watchers asked each person who entered two questions: "Are you a delegate?" and "Are you under thirty?" As it turned out, the crowd control was unnecessary; only eighty young people showed up. This group split into hostile factions of McGovern and non-McGovern delegates, who argued with each other over whether the Youth Caucus ought to endorse a candidate. Some of the young McGovern supporters wanted an endorsement for their candidate, but the Senator's organization was against this. Finally, Chairman Farmer recessed the meeting and reconstituted it as an ad hoc committee to enable a series of speakers to denounce President Nixon and his policies.[12]

On Wednesday, there was a meeting of about thirty-five young delegates who were angry about the poor organization and poor notices of the youth meetings. They passed a unanimous resolution that the group should see Senator McGovern and National Chairman Larry O'Brien to complain about the situation. A delegation of eight young delegates met with McGovern aide Rick Stearns to complain about the Senator's controversial statement on leaving troops in Thailand. They also saw the McGovern research director, John Holum, who had written the speech. Behind the rostrum on Wednesday evening, a small group of youth leaders detailed their complaints to O'Brien: transportation was not available to caucuses; the Connecticut credentials challenge for more young people (only two of the fifty-one delegates were under thirty) had been scrapped; and there were no young people on the podium. O'Brien acceded to the group's demand for a caucus room off the convention floor for Wednesday night.

Youth Caucus members differed on when to hold the meeting; should it be before or after the nomination of the Presidential candidate? Some young delegates talked of breaking their commitments to McGovern because of their anger over his Thailand statement. The meeting, which attracted most of the young delegates, was held before the nomination. But the only resolution passed by the caucus was one committing the group to maintain a continuing organization of youth delegates. One person who attended the meeting commented, "Joe Farmer took control of that meeting. He explained that the role of the Caucus was not to endorse candidates." The McGovern organization began to breathe easier—that meeting of young delegates was the last.

We saw, in the case of the Black Caucus, that there was a growing divergence of perceptions between the white and black delegates about the importance of the caucus. A similar pattern is evident with respect to the Youth Caucus. At the outset of the convention, delegates over thirty-five were slightly more inclined than those under thirty-five to view the Youth Caucus as a site of the most important convention decisions. By Thursday and Friday, however, the young delegates had markedly increased their estimate of the importance of the caucus, while the older delegates moved in the opposite direction. Of the delegates under thirty-five, 44 percent viewed the Youth Caucus as an important arena; of those over thirty-five only 10 percent did so. (See Table 3. The age of thirty-five, rather than thirty, was used as a cutoff point in order to assure adequate sample size in both groups. There was no evidence of differences between the attitudes of those under thirty and those who were thirty to thirty-five.)

The growth in young delegates' estimates of the importance of the caucus was not a gradual one; rather, as Figure 1 shows, there was a sharp increase on Thursday and Friday. It is important to note that this increase followed the Youth Caucus meeting on Wednesday night, which attracted a majority of the young delegates. Indeed, this was the only Youth Caucus event that was well attended. It is possible that the meeting, although it did not produce any major action,

Arenas of Decision

TABLE 3. Percentages of Young and Older Delegates Who Believed Youth Caucus to Be Most Important Arena *

	Young delegates (under 35)	Older delegates (over 35)
Sunday–Monday	16% (6)	20% (11)
Tuesday–Wednesday	15% (4)	18% (8)
Thursday–Friday	44% (11)	10% (3)

* Number of cases upon which percentage is based is included in parentheses. Chi-square probability for young delegates is .018; for older delegates, .524.

raised the importance of the Youth Caucus in the eyes of young delegates.[13]

THE LATIN CAUCUS. About 150 delegates attended a Latin Caucus meeting on Monday. Consisting largely of Chicanos from California and the southwest and of Puerto Ricans from New York, the Latin Caucus discussed ways of making its presence felt at the convention and in the country. The group focused on support of the lettuce boycott and enlisted the help of numerous non-Latin allies in dramatizing this issue. Television viewers were to hear such announcements as "Illinois, the state which is banning the use of lettuce, is proud to cast its votes for. . . ."

THE SENIOR CITIZENS' CAUCUS. The senior citizens, almost a forgotten group at the convention, had planned to hold a caucus of their own on Monday. But the caucus had to be called off when the Presidential candidates, who were to address the senior citizens, held a caucus of their own on the credentials issue.[14]

THE JEWISH CAUCUS. A number of Jewish delegates got together for a caucus on Thursday, July 13, at the Deauville Hotel. Predictably, Middle-East policy was the central concern of the caucus. One delegate who participated com-

FIGURE 1.

Percentages of Young Delegates Who Believed Youth Caucus to Be Most Important Arena

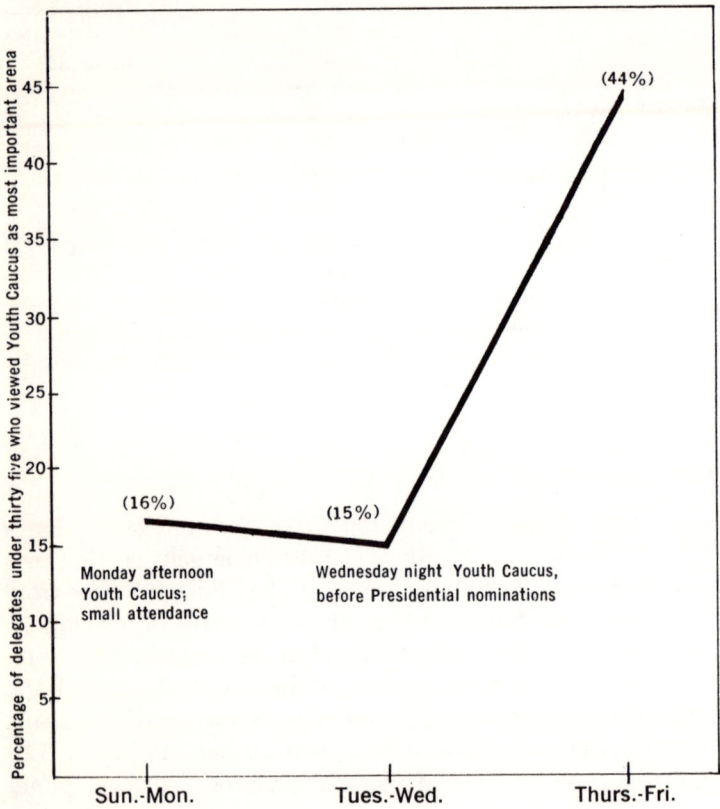

mented, "You know how it was. They complained that McGovern wasn't good enough on Israel."

Now that we have seen some of the activities of the special caucuses during convention week, let us examine some underlying and recurring organizational difficulties with which the caucuses wrestled.

Organizational Problems of the Caucus

TIME. Because of the fast pace and heavy workload of the

convention itself, delegates were pressed for time, and they often could not afford the time to go to special caucus meetings. A common response was, "I would have liked to go to _____ caucus, but I just didn't have the time to get over there." Caucus leaders and participants found that there was not enough time to carry out the grand strategies that some of them had planned. Some members of the Black Caucus had sought to hammer out a common program, see who the front runners were, and then bargain with them in the interests of black people. All this was to be done at the convention, but as Walter Fauntroy, who supported McGovern before the convention, told a news conference, "We looked and saw we couldn't wait that long." [15]

DISTANCE. Related to the problem of time was that of distance. The public transportation facilities in Miami were criticized by many delegates, some of whom cited lack of transportation as the reason why they did not attend group caucuses. The large, liberal McGovern delegations from New York, California, and Massachusetts, whose members might have been expected to play an important role in the special caucuses, were housed far away from the convention center and the headquarters hotels.

DEFINITION OF GROUP. It was not always easy for a group to define itself. Who, for instance, should be allowed into a Women's Caucus: All women delegates? Members of the National Women's Political Caucus? Women who subscribed to certain goals, such as the easing of abortion laws? We have seen that the Black Caucus tried to restrict its membership to delegates and alternates but found it impossible to keep nondelegates out. Finally all black people were let into the meetings of the Black Caucus, with full voting privileges. Nondelegates, who soon constituted a majority, were voting on instructions that were presumably binding on delegates. (These instructions were not closely followed, to say the least.) Thus, the problem of maintaining boundaries around a group proved to be a difficult one.

INTERNAL DISUNITY. If the definition of a group is broad, then the heterogeneity of the group may result in so much internal bickering that action is effectively impeded. For example, there had been a number of black "unity meetings" during the spring that produced a series of different platforms—all in the name of black unity. Some black leaders identified with the National Black Political Agenda that resulted from the Gary meeting, while others based their demands on the Black Bill of Rights from the Congressional Black Caucus. Julian Bond remarked at the convention, "what went wrong from the beginning was that the call for unity came out of Gary, but many of the people who went to Gary are not here." [16]

Presidential politics caused further fragmentation in black unity. Julian Bond observed that "there was a struggle over who was to be the broker for blacks. Mrs. Chisholm wanted to eliminate Walter Fauntroy and others and substitute herself. Some leaders wanted to eliminate her, and Imamu Baraka wanted to eliminate all of them." [17] The strategy of meeting, working out a common platform, and then negotiating with candidates had sounded like a promising one, but individual factions differed sharply over what should constitute the "unity" platform and who should be the negotiator. Before taking on the outside world, the caucuses first had to deal with internal disunity.

CONFLICTS WITH THE GOALS OF OTHER ORGANIZATIONS. A final, critical problem for the special caucuses was that other organizations—notably candidate organizations—felt their own goals might be threatened by the existence of strong, independent group caucuses. The McGovern organization, for example, had serious reservations about an active Youth Caucus. A youth organizer remarked: "Quite frankly, the McGovern organization was reluctant to have an independent Youth Caucus. They felt that it would be bad for McGovern to be attacked from the Left." Thus, McGovern aides tried to discourage the Senator's youth delegates from building an independent caucus. But the aides had to be careful in addressing the activist youth: a young delegate who had observed McGovern staff members talking to the Monday morning caucus of McGovern youth delegates recalled, "It was tough. They really couldn't say—and didn't say—that an independent youth organization would be hazardous. But they strongly *implied* that the first business of the delegates should be the nomination of Senator McGovern."

There were a number of clashes between McGovern aides and leaders of the Women's Caucus. On the South Carolina challenge, some of the caucus activists expressed bitterness about being "sacrificed" in a parliamentary maneuver. And on the abortion issue, tempers flared between McGovern floor managers, who felt that inclusion of the abortion plank would embarrass McGovern, and Women's Caucus leaders, who were fighting for the plank.

The McGovern organization also found itself in conflict with those who wanted to make the Black Caucus an independent locus of decision making. As the front runner, McGovern was wary of any strategy that would lead delegates to break their previous commitments to a candidate. The Humphrey organization, however, had a very different perspective. Running considerably behind in the delegate count, the Humphrey people were eager to implement a strategy that would upset the existing pattern of commitments. If they could encourage the Black Caucus to support Mrs. Chisholm on the first ballot, then some of the blacks supporting McGovern might leave their candidate. This strategy was designed to utilize "black unity" to drive down the McGovern total so that it would fall short of a majority.

Conflicts were not restricted to those between candidate organizations and group caucuses; there were sometimes marked differences among the various caucuses as well. The Latin Caucus, for example, hotly disputed the Women's Caucus stand on liberalized abortion. It would be inaccurate, however, to portray the special caucuses and candidate organizations as bounded units. In fact, there was much overlapping among the organizations. One delegate might be a member of more than one caucus. And, often, caucus members were involved in candidate organizations in addition to their caucus activities. (The black, women's, and youth caucuses, for example, were filled largely by active McGovern supporters.)

For delegates with multiple group identities, there were internal strains. A young man who was active in both the McGovern organization and the National Youth Caucus remarked:

The leaders of the National Youth Caucus were really cross-pressured. The whole organization collapsed before Miami. We started as an organization of liberal young delegates trying to span the candidates. But it didn't make sense, because they were all McGovern delegates. We felt that we should not compete with McGovern—and the McGovern people didn't want us to. They told the National Youth Caucus that the Connecticut challenge was disruptive, and they were concerned that it not become a cause célèbre. They put the pressure on.

Discussing issues before the convention, a number of leaders of the National Women's Political Caucus admitted to being cross-pressured by their loyalties to McGovern and to women. Audrey Beck, a Connecticut state legislator, declared: "At this point I'm a McGovern supporter first because in the last analysis women will get better treatment under McGovern in the next four years than under anybody else." [18] Other women —like Representative Bella Abzug—tended to resolve the conflict in favor of their loyalty to the Women's Caucus.

The special group caucuses were confronted with a number of serious organizational problems: time, distance, group self-definition, internal disunity, and conflicts with the goals of other organizations. It is not surprising that they found it difficult to promulgate common lists of demands and then bargain with candidates and party leaders to further the acceptance of those demands.

The Many Functions of State Delegations

In contrast to the caucuses, the state delegations had a number of advantages as arenas for delegate activity and decision making. Members of state delegations were housed together in Miami Beach; they had been selected at common conventions or in primaries back home; and, often, the delegates had often known each other prior to the national convention.

Delegates had to attend state caucuses to receive their floor credentials and guest passes for the gallery. As one young delegate observed:

State delegations are important. They have meetings

every day. You have to pick up your credential meetings. In group caucuses, you discuss all things. You keep yourselves together and bridge the gaps. But in state delegation caucuses, the business there is the business of the convention. If a youth or women's or black caucus did something you didn't like, you could leave. But you couldn't leave your state delegation.

But state delegations were more than just dispensers of credentials and guest passes. In a number of cases they provided the sites for discussion and planning of state political campaigns. Vermont's delegates spent considerable time in Miami Beach planning what turned out to be the successful Democratic campaign for the governorship. The New Hampshire delegation included a candidate for governor, who campaigned vigorously within the delegation for support in the New Hampshire state primary. (Despite his efforts at Miami Beach, however, his primary race was unsuccessful.) And various Connecticut political leaders sought backing from members of that state delegation for their 1974 statewide races. For McGovern delegates from Connecticut, the state delegation served as a good instrument of socialization; they could learn about the state party machinery and also meet liberal activists from other Connecticut cities. Discussions among California delegates centered around national, rather than local, political issues. But local organizing was not forgotten; a group of California delegates planned to meet after the convention to formulate future projects.[19]

Before the convention, it was thought that outside political groups, such as the Black Caucus, would form dominant arenas within the convention environment. But the convention produced evidence of movement in the opposite direction. State delegation groups, working together at the convention, planned to continue their relationship in politics outside Miami. The District of Columbia delegates, for example, agreed to work as a single force within their city's Democratic party.[20]

A final, and crucial, function performed by state delegations was the transmission of messages from candidate organizations to delegates. Delegates who were already committed wanted information on what issues would come before the convention and how their candidate felt about those issues. State delegations, not group caucuses, were the sites where delegates could gain information and instructions. The candidate organizations listed delegates by state and contacted them in their state delegations. State delegation chairmen, in turn, organized delegation meetings around presentations by candidate representatives. In this way, delegates were able to obtain the information they wanted.

The Importance of Candidate Organizations

The importance of candidate organizations at the convention was considerable. Among decision-making arenas at the convention, the McGovern candidate organization was perceived by the delegates to be the most important. Over 50 percent of the delegates viewed the McGovern organization as the site of the most important decisions at the outset of the convention, and that figure rose to over 70 percent by Thursday and Friday. (Delegates who were not supporters of McGovern were even *more* likely than McGovernites at the end of the convention to view the McGovern organization as the most important arena. In contrast, delegates who were not potential members of the black, women's, and youth caucuses viewed these groups as less important arenas as time went on. See Table 4.)

A delegate's affiliation with a candidate organization influenced how he viewed the group caucuses. Table 5 shows that McGovern delegates perceived the caucuses as more important than did non-McGovern delegates and that McGovern delegates started with high expectations (which decreased over time) for the role of caucuses at the convention. These high expectations may reflect the active part played by McGovern supporters in planning the black, women's, and youth caucuses as well as sympathy for an ideology that saw blacks as the best representatives for the views of blacks, women as the best representatives for women, and young people as the best representatives for youth.

The relationship of a delegate to a candidate organization also influenced the way in which he viewed the convention

TABLE 4. Percentages of McGovern and Non-McGovern Delegates Who Believed McGovern Organization to Be Most Important Arena *

	McGovern delegates	Non-McGovern delegates
Sunday–Monday	67% (31)	38% (12)
Tuesday–Wednesday	77% (26)	52% (16)
Thursday–Friday	68% (27)	86% (12)

* Number of cases upon which percentage is based is included in parentheses. Chi-square probability for McGovern delegates is .629; for non-McGovern delegates, .011.

itself. As time went on, non-McGovern delegates drastically decreased their estimates of the importance of the convention floor as a key decision arena and became much more likely to take the position that "all important decisions were made before the convention." McGovern delegates showed little change with respect to either the relative importance of the convention floor or the assertion that important decisions were made beforehand. (See Table 6.) It is easy to understand why the losing side would take the position that the convention was not really "open," that important decisions were not made on the floor, and that things had really been decided beforehand. As an anti-McGovern delegation chairman said after the crucial California vote, "We're up against a stacked deck." [21]

Conclusions

Although special group caucuses—for blacks, women, and youth, among others—did meet at the 1972 Democratic convention, they faced recurring organizational problems that hindered the achievement of their goals. Some of these problems were related to features of this particular convention; delegates had little time and were often unable to travel the long distances to group caucus meetings.

But other, more general problems could not be explained

TABLE 5. Percentages of McGovern and Non-McGovern Delegates Who Believed Each Caucus to Be Most Important Arena *

	BLACK CAUCUS		WOMEN'S CAUCUS		YOUTH CAUCUS	
	McGovern	Non-McGovern	McGovern	Non-McGovern	McGovern	Non-McGovern
Sunday–Monday	41% (19)	16% (5)	30% (14)	9% (3)	28% (13)	9% (3)
Tuesday–Wednesday	15% (5)	26% (8)	18% (6)	16% (5)	17% (6)	19% (6)
Thursday–Friday	23% (9)	7% (1)	18% (7)	7% (1)	22% (9)	36% (5)

* Number of cases upon which percentage is based is included in parentheses. Chi-square probabilities are:
McGovern delegates–Black Caucus: .021
Non-McGovern delegates–Black Caucus: .286
McGovern delegates–Women's Caucus: .259
Non-McGovern delegates–Women's Caucus: .601
McGovern delegates–Youth Caucus: .539
Non-McGovern delegates–Youth Caucus: .099

TABLE 6. Percentages of McGovern and Non-McGovern Delegates Who Believed All Important Decisions Had Been Made Before Convention, Versus Those Who Believed Convention Floor Was Most Important Arena *

	NON-MC GOVERN DELEGATES		MC GOVERN DELEGATES	
	All decided before convention	Convention floor most important	All decided before convention	Convention floor most important
Sunday–Monday	6% (2)	22% (7)	17% (8)	22% (10)
Tuesday–Wednesday	16% (5)	26% (8)	15% (5)	12% (4)
Thursday–Friday	29% (11)	0% (0)	15% (6)	18% (7)

* Number of cases upon which percentage is based is included in parentheses. Chi-square probabilities are:
Non-McGovern delegates—"all decided before": .126
Non-McGovern delegates—"convention floor": .115
McGovern delegates—"all decided before": .942
McGovern delegates—"convention floor": .515

by the pace and setting of this convention. For example, the groups had difficulty in defining their membership; and if the definition of a group was too broad, there was a risk of internal disunity. Perhaps the most critical problem for the group caucuses was that their goals were sometimes in conflict with those of other organizations, notably candidate organizations. Delegates who had a stake in the nomination of a particular candidate were unlikely to drop their commitment to that candidate in favor of loyalty to a group caucus.

The state delegations, not the group caucuses, were the vehicles through which candidate organizations communicated with delegates. In addition to performing various service functions and facilitating activity relating to local campaigns, state delegations formed the sites where candidate organizations provided information and instructions to delegates. The McGovern organization, which was perceived by delegates as the most important decision-making arena at the convention, listed and contacted delegates through the state delegations. Thus, it was difficult for the group caucuses to compete successfully with state delegations for the time and attention of delegates.

NOTES

1. See, for example, Aaron B. Wildavsky, "What Can I Do? The Ohio Delegate's View of the Convention," in Paul Tillett, ed., *Inside Politics: The National Conventions* (Dobbs Ferry, N.Y.: Oceana Publications, 1960), pp. 112–30.

2. See Paul T. David, Ralph M. Goldman, and Richard C. Bain, *The Politics of National Party Conventions* (Washington, D.C.: Brookings, 1959); Nelson W. Polsby and Aaron B. Wildavsky, "Uncertainty and Decision-Making at the National Conventions," in Nelson W. Polsby, Robert A. Dentler, and Paul A. Smith, eds., *Politics and Social Life* (Boston: Houghton Mifflin, 1963); and Nelson W. Polsby and Aaron B. Wildavsky, *Presidential Elections* (New York: Scribner's, 1971).

3. The Democratic unit rule required that the entire vote of a state delegation be cast as the majority of the delegation desired, if the state delegation had been so instructed by the state convention.

Arenas of Decision

Thus, the unit rule was not imposed on the state delegation by the national convention; rather, the national convention enforced the instructions of the state party. During this century, the importance of the rule had diminished. See V. O. Key, Jr., *Politics, Parties, and Pressure Groups,* 5th ed. (New York: Thomas Y. Crowell, 1964), p. 428.

4. For example, see "Caucus Calling Meeting July 9 of Black Democratic Delegates," *New York Times,* 14 June 1972.

5. Andrea Wolfman, a student at Smith College, provided valuable assistance by writing on the Black Caucus. Ms. Wolfman was a member of the Dartmouth-Berkeley Convention Study Group and also served in Miami as the recording secretary of the Black Caucus. She provided descriptions of the meetings and a number of useful interpretive insights. Michael Hollis, a Dartmouth student, also wrote a useful report on the Black Caucus.

6. Delegates were asked: "Where do you think the most important decisions were made or will be made concerning [delegate's convention goal]?" Respondents were permitted to check the names of as many different arenas as they wished.

7. "Party Selects Woman as National Chairman," *New York Times,* 15 July 1972.

8. See "Women Split on Party Issues," *Washington Post,* 10 July 1972.

9. "Women Boo as McGovern Skirts Their Issues," *Washington Post,* 11 July 1972.

10. Ibid.

11. The McGovern organization supported the South Carolina challenge, but it wanted to ensure that the winning total on the vote did not fall between a majority of those voting and an absolute majority of the total number of delegates. If such an outcome had occurred, the anti-McGovern forces could have appealed the result and called for a test vote on convention voting rules at a time when McGovern's delegate strength was comparatively low. In order to avoid this parliamentary situation, McGovern leaders, uncertain of their ability to win by an absolute majority, asked some of their delegates to vote "no" instead of "yes" on the challenge. Thus, the vote was lost but—since the opponents' winning total was more than an absolute majority of all delegates—the parliamentary appeal could not be made.

12. See "Caucuses Are Bound by Common Identity," *New York Times*, 11 July 1972.

13. Another possible explanation for the increase was that students (who constitute a larger percentage of the Thursday-Friday sample than they do of other days) were more inclined to view the Youth Caucus as important. But students and nonstudents were found not to differ on this question.

14. "Caucuses Are Bound by Common Identity," op. cit.

15. "In Waning Hours, Mrs. Chisholm Courted 1st Ballot Support," *Washington Post*, 13 July 1972.

16. "Blacks Are Divided on the Convention," *New York Times*, 16 July 1972.

17. Ibid.

18. "Women Split on Party Issues," op. cit.

19. The discussion of particular delegations is based on a series of state delegation reports that were prepared as part of the convention study. John Lyons reported on New Hampshire, Kate Pressman on Connecticut, Denis Sullivan on Vermont, and Jeffrey Pressman on California.

20. See "Fauntroy Increases Party Role," *Washington Post*, 14 July 1972.

21. "We Face 'Stacked Deck,' State Delegate Chief Says," *Miami Herald*, 12 July 1972.

chapter four

Innovation and Compromise
The Making of a Party Platform

· · · · · · · · · · · · · · · · ·

In 1972 the "new politics" of George McGovern captured control of the national convention of the Democratic party. *For the People,* the platform approved by that convention, was in many ways an interesting and even inspiring document. It recited the ills of America—continuation of the ugly war in Vietnam, neglect of the poor and the black and the brown, high unemployment, rising prices, high taxes, widespread cynicism and despair about politics. Without denying some Democratic responsibility for these problems, it proclaimed a sweeping set of solutions: an immediate end to the war by complete American withdrawal, a restructuring of taxation to redistribute income, new openness to the poor and minorities.

How seriously should one take this (or any) platform? Did the delegates care about it? What about the content of this particular platform? Did it really chart dramatic new political directions, or did it merely echo Democratic platforms of the past? Did it offer practical guides to legislation or just vague sentiments? Finally, how did it come about? What parts do interest groups, candidates, and delegates play in writing a platform, and with what aims?

Does It Matter?

The issue stands of political parties occupy a central place in theories of democratic control of policy making. To Anthony

Downs and others, elections ensure popular control through a process of anticipated reactions in which politicians choose the issue stands most pleasing to the public in order to win votes. *Both* parties in a two-party system tend to take similar stands, close to what the public wants. The party that wins presumably enacts its programs and reflects the popular will.[1]

"Responsible party" theorists also consider issue stands important but in a different context. They see the issue stands of parties as calls to arms, as efforts to mobilize support for conflicting views of what ought to be done. Each party tries to persuade citizens of the virtue of its own stands; on election day the voters choose between the two packages of policy, and the winning party—the party with the more popular program —proceeds to enact its policies.[2]

If the issue stands of parties are important, then so, one must assume, are party platforms. How else do parties as a whole express their views? In the decentralized American political system, only the platform brings together all factions of the party and reflects a synthesis of all views. Only the platform is an institutional product of the whole party.

One might object, of course, that neither Downsian nor responsible party theories of democratic control have much relation to reality in America. It may happen that parties will *not* take issue stands in response to popular will; people may not perceive the stands correctly, or at all, and they may not be persuaded by them or vote on the basis of them. Above all, what a party does in office may differ drastically from what it promises in an election campaign. Officials may feel free to disregard campaign pledges, or even if they wish to keep their promises, they may be thwarted by competing centers of power. Furthermore, whatever the importance of parties' issue stands, the platform may be far less important and less visible than the speeches of Presidential candidates, which make their way directly into the homes of citizens via newspapers and television.

Taken to its extreme, this objection holds that platforms are completely insignificant. Certainly it is true that few convention delegates read them. In 1972, even though the platform had been sent to all delegates ten days before the convention, most of those interviewed admitted that they had not had time to look at it. Some explicitly denied its importance. When questioned about the platform, one old-line party leader from Connecticut replied with an incredulous stare and finally growled, "Have *you* ever read a platform?" (The questioner had not.) A veteran Missouri labor leader said, "It means nothing. There's only twelve people that read it. The candidate is the platform."

If most convention delegates—who had to vote on the platform and various amendments to it—failed to struggle through the 93 pages (24,000 words) of text, we can be sure that scarcely a handful of ordinary citizens read it. Even the sketchy newspaper and television accounts of the platform, which appeared on a single day in July, must have reached only a small minority of Americans. It would be unreasonable to claim that the platform itself, or direct reports of it, had a strong impact on people's perceptions of party stands or on their voting decisions in November.

Yet many delegates thought the platform important. Fifteen percent went so far as to mention it in connection with "the most important thing" they wanted to see done at the convention. When asked what they wanted to see included (or excluded), 71 percent of the delegates mentioned at least one specific plank, and some mentioned many. (See Table 1.) On the other hand, 11 percent volunteered that the platform was irrelevant, that it made no difference. In our interviews some of the delegates explained why they thought the platform was significant. The reasons they gave shed some light on their thinking and also suggest some functions a platform may serve and some kinds of impact it may have.

A McGovern organizer from Connecticut acknowledged that the platform actually has little direct effect but asserted that it has symbolic value: "And men are moved by symbols." A young New Yorker agreed that the platform is not directly important—in fact, it functions mainly to give ammunition to the other side. But "It sets the tone for the future; it gets people talking. It makes issues respectable." Four years ago, who would have expected an abortion plank to be seriously considered? And four years from now (not foreseeing the Su-

TABLE 1. **Percentages of Delegates Who Mentioned Specific Platform Topics** *

Number of topics mentioned	Percentage of delegates
0	29% (67)
1	24 (56)
2	26 (62)
3	11 (26)
4	6 (13)
5	3 (6)
6	1 (2)
7	1 (2)
	101 (234)

* The delegates were asked what they would like to see excluded from or included in the platform. The number of cases upon which each percentage is based is included in parentheses.

preme Court's action) such a plank will probably be adopted. Once a platform sets the general direction of policy, "Congress can work out the exact wording of legislation."

Even the history professor from North Carolina who was somewhat cynical about platforms—"they are like college catalogue course descriptions: never the same as the course, but designed for appeal"—implied that there was some relation between platforms and policy. Others trustingly felt that "what politicians say, they are likely to do." According to a Chicano community leader from Illinois, "it will be taken into consideration after the man is elected."

There may be some truth to such claims. Gerald Pomper has offered evidence that platforms do tend to become policy.[3] The relationship between political rhetoric and action is complex, and perhaps platforms are nearer to being indicators than causes of future policy making: they reflect the same forces that eventually influence legislation. Yet a platform itself can also be a gateway for new ideas and demands, which may originate with small minorities, to find their way into the political system and win more general acceptance. A platform does "get people talking"—at least political elites—and it does help "make issues respectable."

Occasionally, a party platform may even serve as a comprehensive agenda for future legislation. Such a role is often attributed to the Democratic platform of 1948, which set forth many proposals that were enacted during the 1950s and 1960s.[4]

Moreover, a platform undoubtedly has some indirect effect on popular perceptions and voting choices. The general thrust (which, in 1972, was antiwar, probusing, pro-guaranteed income) is probably communicated to voters by the candidates in their repetitions of it, through media reports of the reactions of reference groups (organized labor, blacks), and in the two-step flow through local opinion leaders. Indeed, the most innovative and controversial planks are likely to be publicized by the opposing party's attacks on them.

Platforms sometimes provide preliminary skirmishing grounds over which candidates for nomination test their strength and try to attract new supporters, as in 1968 when the McCarthy-Kennedy-McGovern forces and the Humphrey forces struggled over the Vietnam plank.[5] As we shall see, however, this was not notably the case in 1972; many platform conflicts in fact pitted McGovern against factions of his own supporters.

Finally, platforms almost always perform an integrative function, as sets of symbols for bringing about harmony among factions and cementing their allegiance to the party. Defeated contenders for the nomination are often appeased by being given a role in the making of the platform: notable examples include Nixon's deference to Rockefeller on the Republican platform of 1960,[6] and Roosevelt's capitulation to Wilsonian progressives (when he let them write the entire platform) in 1932.[7] Interest groups—farmers, labor, business, minorities—are given explicit recognition, and their fondest policy aims are acknowledged. When this maneuver is successful, the platform activates workers and provides a banner of unity that strengthens the party for the upcoming election.

Whatever the objective significance of the platform, we have seen that in 1972 many delegates thought it important. But the degree of importance they attributed to it tended to vary among the supporters of different Presidential candidates in a fashion that revealed something of the changes occurring in the Democratic party. Our interviews showed that McGovern supporters were more issue oriented and somewhat more likely to think that the platform was important than were uncommitted delegates or supporters of Humphrey, Muskie, or Jackson; and Wallace delegates, who had no hope of nominating their man, put the most emphasis of all on the platform.

For many supporters of the traditional candidates, issues did not appear to be crucial. When asked what they liked about the Democratic party, some regulars were hard put to respond. They usually claimed it was the "party of the people" (more than one complained that it *used to be* the party of the people), but beyond that they had little to say about public policy. Responses about "party of the little man" or "party of the people" seemed almost ritualized. Many spoke in terms of organizational loyalty. Some responses were altogether devoid of policy content: "Well, there are only two parties to choose from in the United States, it's not like France. . . . You're born into one, or something, and you stay with it. When you belong to a ball team, you stick by it. Like Dartmouth." (This man had been a state senator for fourteen years and was now President Pro Tem.)

McGovern delegates, on the other hand—both young and old—were vociferously interested in issues. They cared about the Vietnam war, about poverty in America, about sexual and stylistic freedom. Many viewed the party as a vehicle for policy goals, and some refused to commit themselves on future loyalty to it or even to their candidate. "I'm not wedded to McGovern." "Well, if he sells out, I'll have to start a 'dump McGovern' movement."

A few McGovern delegates, especially in the ideologically pure New York, Massachusetts, and California delegations, denied they were Democrats at all. "Democratic Party? Why I've never voted for a Democrat in a general election. . . . I was in the streets in Atlantic City in 1964 and Chicago in 1968. . . ." Even some who were making their careers in the party conditioned their loyalty on policy considerations. Said a young legislator from Connecticut, ". . . it represents the common people, more than the Republican party in most places I happen to have been. . . ." He implied that if he moved to a different state or community, he might find himself a Republican.

The greater issue orientation of McGovern delegates spilled over, to some extent, into concern about the platform. They had more ideas about what should be included in it than did other delegates. Seventy-eight percent of them, contrasted with only 60 percent of the delegates backing the regular candidates, cited at least one issue, and many listed three or four or more.

But this is not to say that McGovern delegates were clamoring to put radical planks in the platform; far from it. For reasons of electoral strategy, many McGovern delegates, and the McGovern organization itself, worked to keep certain strong issue stands *out* of the platform. They feared that extreme platform planks would alienate parts of the electorate and lose votes for McGovern in November. Moreover, the vast majority were more concerned about nominating their candidate than about writing a platform. Giving priority to the nomination was of course quite consistent with their issue orientation, since the McGovern delegates felt they had an issue-oriented candidate with a good chance of victory. Only the Wallace delegates—also issue oriented, but lacking a serious contender for the nomination—tended to mention the adoption of a platform as the most important task of the convention. (See Table 2.)

Nonetheless, there was considerable tension in the McGovern camp between those who placed issues above all and

TABLE 2. Percentages of Delegates Who Considered Platform Important and Unimportant, by Candidate Commitment

Perception of platform *	CANDIDATE COMMITMENT		
	McGovern	Wallace	Other
Important	25%	35%	21%
No mention or unimportant	75	65	79

* Delegates were identified as considering the platform "important" only if they mentioned it in connection with the most important thing they wanted to see done at the convention or volunteered elsewhere that it was important.

those who (even for issue-related reasons) were primarily devoted to nominating and electing a candidate. And individual McGovern delegates themselves were torn between commitment to issues and commitment to the candidate. The conflict between their desires—on the one hand to innovate, to educate, to express their beliefs, and on the other hand to win nomination and election for their standard-bearer, compromising on some issues if necessary—became a major factor in the construction of the platform.

What Did It Say?

The 1972 platform, *For the People,* blended continuity and change. On the one hand, it grew out of and had much in common with the Democratic platforms of 1968 and earlier. On the other hand, it was much longer than the 1968 platform, much more specific, and carried traditional Democratic promises further; it also broached some wholly new questions, and pointed to some new directions where American government might move.

The elements of continuity were strong, particularly concerning those policies which since New Deal days had distinguished the Democrats as the party of the "little man," of federal social-welfare legislation. The platform opened, in fact, with the assertion that "[f]ull employment—a guaranteed job for all—is the primary economic objective. . . ." In addition to stimulation of private enterprise, it prescribed "greatly expanded" public service employment and, like the 1968 platform, declared that the government should be the "employer of last resort" (p. II:4).[8]

The platform also advocated "[a]dequate federal income assistance" for those not benefiting sufficiently from Social Security and the like, and the replacement of the present welfare system by an "income security program" of cash assistance based on an earned income approach, to keep everyone above the poverty level (pp. II:4, 5). This echoed the 1968 commitment to federalize welfare and to provide to every poor American family "assistance free of the indignities and uncertainties that still too often mar our present programs" (p. 48).

On labor-management relations, the 1972 platform promised

to repeal the "open shop" provision in Section XIV-B of the Taft–Hartley Act, to expand unemployment insurance and workmen's compensation, to raise the minimum wage, and to expand coverage of the Fair Labor Standards Act (pp. II:11, 12). The 1968 platform had said much the same things (pp. 33, 46). The chief additions in 1972 were a denunciation of Nixon's proposal for compulsory arbitration of transportation disputes (p. II:11) and hearty support for Cesar Chavez's United Farm Workers, including a call for a boycott of nonunion lettuce (p. II:14).

(This lettuce boycott provision became a great rallying cry at the convention. It pleased the Chicanos, and offended few, lettuce growers being an unrepresented minority—though one outraged conservative from Missouri was heard to mutter that he had just ordered a crate of lettuce and felt consciencebound to eat it all. Delegates on the convention floor vied in their expressions of enthusiasm. Senator Kennedy worked a line about lettuce into his introduction of McGovern. A party regular from Illinois happily blended the old and the new politics by proclaiming that Illinois, too, had decided to "ban the use of lettuce.")

Many proposals touching particular groups also resembled those of the past. As in 1968, the platform called for greater participation by young people in party and convention politics and as candidates for public office; it moved forward from the pledge of eighteen-year-old voting to lowering the age of legal majority and consent to eighteen (p. III:7). It upheld full citizenship rights for American Indians and protection of their land rights; it opposed the termination policy. Going beyond the 1968 position (p. 43), *For the People* (as amended on the convention floor) supported allocation of federal surplus lands to American Indians on a first priority basis (p. MR:6).

The platform called for assistance to the elderly in the form of increases (and automatic inflation adjustments) in Social Security, vesting of pension rights, expansion of housing assistance and Medicare, and federal inspection of and support for nursing homes (pp. III:9, 10). Most of this echoed 1968 (pp. 47–48). It favored "improving and extending" veterans' benefits in medical care, education, and jobs (pp. III:10, 11). In this, too, the 1968 platform is similar (p. 51). It advocated establishment of an independent consumer agency with legal powers, as well as complete product labeling, consumer class actions, and "no fault" insurance (pp. III:12, 13). This went somewhat beyond the 1968 proposals for an Office of Consumer Affairs, which made federal product information available (pp. 34–35).

On health care, the 1968 platform had expressed determination to make medical care available to every American, regardless of economic status; it had called for stemming the rise in medical and drug costs, raising the level of research, building new facilities, and extending Medicare to prenatal and postnatal coverage of mothers and infants (pp. 49–51). In 1972, the platform extended these promises and made them more concrete: it called for a system of Universal National Health Insurance which would give all Americans comprehensive coverage, with built-in incentives and controls to curb inflation in costs; it repeated the call for federal funds to train medical personnel and conduct research; and it specified antitrust and patent law approaches to control of drug prices and supported generic labeling of drugs (pp. III:14–15). In a new departure, it also advocated that family planning services be made available to all (p. III:15).

Like the previous platform (p. 59), *For the People* supported federal revenue sharing with state and local governments, and it put special emphasis on the lively issue of property tax relief. And, as in 1968, it committed the party to reorganization of categorical grant programs (p. IV:4). As before, it called for the construction of a large amount of new housing and the providing of direct low-interest loans for construction and purchase. Again, it supported the building of "New Towns." (See 1968, pp. 35–36.) For the first time, however, it questioned the logic of urban renewal, noting the option of "preservation" of existing neighborhoods. It criticized highway policies that destroy neighborhoods and called for complete overhaul of the F.H.A. to make it consumer oriented (pp. IV:6–9).

On education policy, the 1972 platform, like that of 1968 (p. 52), called for "fully funding" Title I of the Elementary and Secondary Education Act (p. V:2), full funding of school breakfast and lunch programs (p. V:3), increased support for

Innovation and Compromise

bilingual education (pp. V:4–5), full appropriations for vocational education (p. V:5), guaranteed access to loans for all higher education students (p. V:6), and increased support for the arts and humanities (p. V:7). It broke some new ground by advocating equalization of spending among school districts (p. V:2), passage of the Comprehensive Child Development Act which Nixon had vetoed (p. V:3), "transportation" (busing) of children as one tool for desegregation of schools (p. V:4), and long-range financing for public broadcasting to insulate it from political pressures (p. V:7).

On "Crime, Law, and Justice," the platform largely followed that of 1968 (pp. 61–65), though it was freed of the obsession with riots in black ghettoes. *For the People* called for federal assistance to upgrade pay and training of police and an expansion and streamlining of the court system (p. VI:4); it advocated control of handguns, including a complete ban on the sale of "Saturday night specials," increased penalties for narcotics traffickers, and a halt to illegal entry of drugs with a suspension of all aid to noncooperating countries (p. VI:5), and expanded enforcement efforts against organized and white-collar crime (p. VI:6). New directions included an emphasis on rehabilitation of criminals and on rights to privacy.

Farm policy proposals in 1972 were also much the same as those of the past. The platform pledged loans and payments to raise family farm income to 100 percent of parity (p. VII:3). Going beyond the previous half-hearted reference to limiting subsidies for large corporate farms, however, it promised flatly to "end farm program benefits to farm units larger than family size" (p. VII:4). Again it favored creation of a strategic reserve of commodities (p. VII:4), upheld collective bargaining (pp. VII:4–5), and supported the Rural Electrification Administration (p. VII:6). New material included some protectionist language about duties and inspection standards for agricultural imports (p. VII:4), support for the appointment of a farmer or rancher as Secretary of Agriculture (p. VII:5), and a brief recapitulation of support for the United Farm Workers (p. VII:6).

The most clearly innovative aspects of the platform, the most dramatic breaks with the past, concerned foreign affairs. And in foreign policy, the first and most important topic was the

Vietnam war. Here the platform departed sharply from the past and closely followed the proposals of George McGovern and his antiwar followers:

> . . . [W]e pledge, as the first order of business, an immediate and complete withdrawal of all U.S. forces in Indo-China. All U.S. military action in Southeast Asia will cease. After the end of U.S. direct combat participation, military aid to the Saigon government, and elsewhere in Indo-China, will be terminated [pp. VIII:3–4].

The contrast with 1968 was great. In that year, under pressure from Lyndon Johnson, the party completely rejected Eugene McCarthy's proposals and adopted a Vietnam plank that spoke of negotiating an "honorable and lasting settlement" with *mutual* troop withdrawals and free elections: "We reject as unacceptable a unilateral withdrawal of our forces which would allow that aggression and subversion to succeed" (pp. 19–20).

Beyond Vietnam, *For the People* declared that "the military budget can be reduced substantially with no weakening of our national security" (p. VIII:6). This was not as strong as McGovern's mention of a $30 billion cut, but it definitely changed the direction from the 1968 platform, which urged a "strong and balanced defense establishment" and made no commitment to reductions beyond the traditional pledge to continue eliminating "waste and duplication" (p. 17).

The 1972 platform advocated decreases in military commitments and military aid throughout most of the world. It said the next Democratic administration should "[r]educe U.S. troop levels in Europe . . ." (p. VIII:7), whereas the previous platform had spoken merely of larger European contributions to NATO (p. 17). It called for cessation of support for the "repressive Greek military government" (p. VIII:8), sharp reduction in military aid to Africa and a complete stop to military aid for Portugal (p. VIII:9), and sharp reduction in military assistance throughout Latin America, as well as "intervention by military means" (p. VIII:11). Only for Israel was there a strong commitment to provide aircraft and other military equipment, and (after amendment of the foreign policy plank on the convention floor) to maintain "ample" forces in Europe and at sea to deter Soviet pressure on Israel (pp. VIII:4–9, MR:13).

The main thrust of foreign policy proposals was to scale down military involvement, including a general "curtailment of military aid" (p. VIII:14), a negotiated ban on all nuclear testing, and ratification of the Protocol on Chemical Warfare without reservation (p. VIII:7).

At the same time, however, the platform was far from isolationist. It advocated increased humanitarian intervention abroad, especially in the third world; expanded economic aid to Africa; support for UN control over Namibia (South West Africa); vigorous support for UN sanctions against racist Rhodesia, specifically on the issue of chrome imports; and pressure for justice for black employees of U.S. firms in South Africa (p. VIII:9). It pledged "generous" support for the reconstruction of Bangla Desh, serious negotiations on trade and exchanges with China and steps to establish diplomatic relations, and assistance to economic development in Asia (p. VIII:10), as well as "humanitarian assistance" to the people of Vietnam (p. VII:4). It proposed that the United States reexamine relations with Cuba and reestablish a U.S.–Mexico border commission (p. VIII:11). It called for increased UN activity and involvement in world problems and repeal of the Connally Reservation on jurisdiction of the World Court (p. VIII:12). Only in the field of international trade were there hints of isolationism—while proclaiming adherence to "liberal trade policies" and advocating reciprocal reductions of barriers, the platform complained of unfair competition due to low wages and working standards abroad (p. VIII:13). But for the most part, the platform urged a new direction of humanitarian intervention and military restraint in foreign policy.

The foreign affairs decision-making process itself was subject to two recommendations: "Greater sharing with Congress of real decisions on issues of war and peace"; and "More honest information policies," including reform of document classification and regular press conferences by the President and senior officials (p. VIII:14).

In the realm of domestic affairs, as we have noted, many of the platform's innovations simply moved one more step down the established path of the Democratic party, or modified the direction slightly. The proposal for Universal National Health Insurance was of this type—a culmination of years of proposals for federal help with medical care. The hints of protectionism in agriculture—duties to prevent "unfair competition," "rigid standards" for inspection of meat and dairy imports (p. VII:4)—and in trade generally (p. VIII:13), did not stray far from traditional Democratic free-trade stands. The strong support for Chavez's United Farm Workers and even the lettuce boycott (pp. II:11–14, VII:6) could be read as simply fleshing out the 1968 support for collective bargaining in agriculture (p. 31) and application of the National Labor Relations Act to farm workers (p. 33). The passage on rehabilitation of prisoners built upon 1968's brief allusion to rehabilitation (p. 63).

Even on the matter of tax reform, the platform had roots in the past. The 1968 platform had pledged "major reliance on progressive taxes," and promised a "thorough revamping" of federal taxes to make them more equitable between rich and poor: "all corporation and individual preferences that do not serve the national interest should be removed" (pp. 27–28). From one point of view, the 1972 platform merely expanded on this commitment and became more specific.

At some point, however, incremental changes cumulate into something more; quantitative changes become qualitative. In this sense, *For the People* must be read as signaling some major shifts in old policies and raising some new issues that had scarcely appeared in national politics before. In addition to the turning away from military involvement abroad, which we have already described (and which might be labeled neo-isolationism), there were three types of broad changes: (1) populism—revitalized opposition to big business, and advocacy of a redistribution of wealth and power, (2) postindustrial values—enunciation of new rights and values concerning the environment, privacy, and governmental openness, and (3) participation—the inclusion of new, previously ignored groups in the politics of party and nation.

The *Wall Street Journal* headlined the proposed Democratic platform of 1972 as "Unfriendly to Big Business" (28 June 1972). That was, if anything, an understatement. The platform declared that the government should "Step up anti-trust action to help competition, with particular regard to laws and enforcement curbing conglomerate mergers which swallow up efficient small business and feed the power of corporate giants" (p. II:7). It "deplore[d] the increasing concentration of economic power in fewer and fewer hands." It said the government should "[s]trengthen the anti-trust laws" to break up large conglomerates, abolish the oil import quota, "[d]econcentrate shared monopolies such as auto, steel and tire industries," and "[s]tiffen the civil and criminal statutes to make corporate officers responsible for their actions" (p. II:708). In contrast, the 1968 platform had devoted only one sentence to these matters, pledging to "[s]trictly enforce anti-trust and trade practice laws . . ." (p. 29).

As we have seen, the platform promised flatly to "end" farm program benefits to farm units larger than family size (p. VII:4). It went on to pledge to "prohibit farming, or the gaining of monopolistic control of production, on the part of corporations whose resources and income derive primarily from non-farm sources," "[t]o investigate violations and enforce anti-trust laws in corporation-agriculture-agribusiness interlocks," and to "prohibit corporations and individuals from setting up tax shelters or otherwise engaging in agriculture primarily for the purpose of tax avoidance or tax loss" (p. VII:5).

Further, the platform condemned the federal tax system as "grossly unfair": "The wealthy and corporations get special tax favors; some require major reform of the nation's tax structure—to achieve a more equitable distribution of income . . ." (p. II:8). It called progressive taxation "all but a dead letter" (p. II:10).

On the federal income tax, it declared that "all unfair corporate and individual tax preferences should be removed." It cited "complicated provisions and special interests" that clogged the law, such as the oil depletion allowance, special rates for capital gains, fast depreciation, easy to abuse "expense-account" deductions, and the "ineffective" minimum tax. It endorsed, as a "minimum step," the Mills-Mansfield proposal to repeal and review virtually all preferences, and it declared that the "most unjustified loopholes should be closed immediately," without waiting for review (p. II:9).

For the People committed the party to "make the Social Security tax progressive" by raising substantially the ceiling on "earned" income and by using general revenues to supplement payroll tax receipts. It proposed reducing the burden of local property taxes through federal revenue sharing (p. II:10).

These proposed tax reforms were left a bit vague, and did not extend as far as McGovern's original proposal to raise $17 billion in new revenues or Harris's minority plank, but they still went well beyond the pieties of 1968 (pp. 27–28).

A second major theme of the platform was that of bringing new groups into the political system. Since New Deal days, the Democratic party has promised benefits to working people, the poor, and (at least since 1948) blacks. The 1972 platform continued that tradition. Tax reform, guaranteed jobs, income assistance, and all the social welfare proposals were intended to help the little man. But the platform also reached out to groups that had previously played little part in politics and had received little recognition: women, young people, Chicanos, Indians, even prisoners.

Women made a dramatic entrance into Democratic politics in 1972; under the new rules for delegate selection, which imposed quotas by sex, they constituted about 40 percent of the delegates, compared to a previous 15 percent. The platform reflected their new importance. Whereas the 1968 platform scarcely mentioned the word "women" at all, *For the People* devoted a long section to this group. It called for a "priority effort" to ratify the Equal Rights Amendment, elimination of discrimination in jobs and public accommodations, extension of the jurisdiction of the Civil Rights Commission to cover women, opening educational equality, making maternity benefits available to all working women, eliminating tax inequities and permitting deduction of housekeeping and childcare costs as business expenses, extension of the Equal Pay Act to cover all workers, and appointment of women to top government positions (pp. III:6–7).

At the convention there was strong sentiment among women to override McGovern's wishes by adding a provision that, in matters of sexual reproduction, each person's right to privacy and freedom of choice should be fully respected—rather mild language that was interpreted as favoring liberalized abortion laws (p. MR:7). But the McGovern organization was able to convince a sufficient number of McGovern delegates that their candidate's chance for election would be hurt by the inclusion of such a platform plank, and it was defeated. The delegates did make a woman, "Sissy" Farenthold, a runner-up for the Vice-Presidential nomination, and they elected a woman as national chairman of the party.

Young people, who had contributed most of the troops to McGovern's political crusade, saw efforts to lower the age of legal majority and consent to eighteen and to encourage and assist the election of young people to government office (p. III:7), which derived from the promises of 1968. Perhaps more important to politically active young people, the platform urged abolition of the draft (p. VIII:8) and stated a "firm intention" to declare an amnesty, "on an appropriate basis," to those who for reasons of conscience refused to serve in the Vietnam war and were prosecuted or sought refuge abroad (p. VIII:4). Amnesty was a shining symbol for McGovern's young campaigners, and it was included in the platform despite unease among traditional Democrats and fears of Republican attacks. But the youth, like women, lost one important battle; the legalization of marijuana issue was viewed as too hot to handle and was dropped at the Platform Committee stage.

The platform specified many "rights of children," including child-care programs, medical care, and education; it favored revision of the juvenile court system and allocation of funds to provide counsel in juvenile proceedings (p. III:5).

For American Indians, the platform repeated old promises of full citizenship, federal aid, and preservation of land rights (p. III:8); as amended, it went further and supported "allocation of federal surplus lands" to Indians on a first-priority basis (p. MR:9). Blacks were not given a special section—it almost seemed as if there was a mutual effort to make black "demands" less visible—but the planks on busing, guaranteed jobs, and income maintenance were highly responsive to their desires. In addition, minority planks on rent control (p. MR:6) and on a guaranteed income of $6,500 for a family of four (p. MR:5), which had heavy black support, were seriously considered on the convention floor. In 1972 blacks were no longer seeking recognition as a group; they sought general economic measures that would benefit blacks along with all the poor.

For Chicanos, the platform endorsed Cesar Chavez and the United Farm Workers by name and called for the lettuce boycott; these had been the single-minded aims of the Latin Caucus and provided symbolic recognition for the group, which was reinforced every time a delegate on the convention floor invoked the magic word "lettuce" (pp. II:13–14).

Even prisoners were offered a variety of rights in a section on "rehabilitation" that far overshadowed the brief allusion to the issue in 1968 (p. 63). The platform called for restoration after a prisoner's release of rights to drivers' licenses, employment, the vote, and office holding. It advocated more community-based rehabilitation facilities, especially for juveniles, and work-release furlough programs. Within the prisons, it called for recognition of the "constitutional and human rights" of prisoners and for "realistic therapeutic, vocational, wage-earning, education, alcoholism, and drug treatment programs" (p. VI:7). Finally, one of the most marginal groups in American society—homosexuals—came close to receiving recognition in the "gay liberation" minority plank, which outlined an array of antidiscrimination provisions, but which was defeated on the convention floor (p. MR:8).

Without question, the platform was responsive to new groups, particularly women and young people, who had been brought into political activity by the reform rules and the McGovern candidacy. In fact, the emphasis on the new groups was even greater than it would appear from platform language alone; it was precisely the language concerning those groups, and efforts to go farther in meeting their policy preferences, that occupied most of the time and attention of delegates during the session on the platform. Slogans about lettuce filled the air; there was intense debate and lobbying about abortion, Indian land, the $6,500 income, and gay liberation. Particularly when the platform is viewed in the light of convention debate, it reflects the changing nature of the Democratic party—the move away from organized labor and toward the "new minorities" including middle-class, politically active women and young people.

A third major theme in the platform was enunciation of new issues and values. Environmental concerns, for example, received so much more attention than in 1968, that they could be called genuinely new. The calls for federal funding of waste management and purification of air and water (p. IV: 10); for strict enforcement of air pollution standards and a cessation of harmful discharge into our waters by 1985 (p. IV:11); for agreement on an international accord for the seas (p. IV:14); and for more funds for expansion of national seashores, parks, riverways, and wilderness reserves (pp. IV: 15–16) all grew from similar pledges in 1968 (pp. 55–58). In 1972, however, they were carried farther and a new sense of urgency was added to them. For the first time, the urban renewal philosophy of destruction and rebuilding was challenged (pp. IV:7, 8). The dictatorship of the automobile was questioned, and the platform recommended replacing the Highway Trust Fund with a single Transportation Trust Fund that could be used for mass transit as well as for roads (p. IV:9).

Another important departure in the platform was the lengthy discussion of the "right to be different," rights to privacy, the right to be left alone by government. Perhaps because the incumbent party tends to be less skeptical of governmental power than does its opposition, the Democratic convention of 1968 had not concerned itself with such matters. *For the People* criticized wiretapping, electronic surveillance, and the use of grand juries for political intimidation. It strongly objected to secret computer data banks on individuals, maintaining that people should have access to their files and the right to insert corrective material. It rejected the idea of a National Computer Data Bank (p. III:2).

Perhaps the most insistent new theme was the call for greater openness and wider public participation in government. The platform called for a more responsive Democratic party in Congress—for using the powers of the House and Senate caucuses to implement party programs by choosing responsive committee chairmen and by disciplining committee members. It called for "open meetings" legislation barring secrecy even in committee sessions for drafting bills, for individual recording and public availability of all committee and floor votes, for reservation of executive privilege to the President alone, for strengthening the Freedom of Information Act and requiring annual reports on all refusals to grant information, and for more systematic declassification of documents (pp. IX:2–4).

In administrative proceedings, the platform recommended that all communications between an agency and outside parties about pending decisions be written and made public (implicitly alluding to the ITT case), that conflict of interest laws should apply, that consent decrees should be publicized ninety days before submission, and that the Justice Department should report annually its actions on major suits (pp. IX:4–5).

The platform also called for public financing of most election costs by 1974 and a statutory ceiling on political gifts. It asked for full disclosure of the financial interests of members of Congress, their staffs, and high executive and administrative officials, as well as a ban on the practice of law by Congressmen while in office, and it recommended that rigorous lobbying disclosure legislation be enacted (pp. IX:5–6).

For the People sought to promote direct involvement in politics through several methods: by providing financial assistance to convention delegates; through universal voter registration by post card, liberalized absentee voting, residency requirements of thirty days or less for all elections, students' voting at their schools, and lower minimum ages for service in the Senate and House (p. IX:7). This theme of openness and participation, of course, meshed neatly with the effort to bring particular new groups into the party and political system.

Taken as a whole, *For the People* could certainly not be called radical. Much of it followed naturally from long-standing commitments of the Democratic party. Even what was new did not stray far from the mainstream of American politics, and in some cases it may have followed, rather than led, trends in public opinion. Since 1968, public concern with the environment had grown, disillusionment with the Vietnam war was practically complete, the women's movement surged, there were stirrings of populism—based chiefly on resentment of high taxes, and people had come to want less government surveillance and more openness and participation. To some degree, the innovations of the platform were simply responses to new desires of the people.

The roles of leader and follower in politics are often hard to disentangle; politicians are skillful at saying what people want to hear. But we can be sure that the platform was *not* solely an echo of popular opinion. It set forth a number of interesting specific solutions to what were only vague concerns for most citizens. In many cases, the proposals went beyond what public opinion polls revealed as the current orthodoxies, and they certainly went beyond current legislation or the Republican platform. The Democratic platform, as we shall see, arose out of an interplay between what politicians thought was "good" policy, and what they thought would win votes. The result was not a manifesto for the complete restructuring of American society, but *For the People* did contain some significant innovative thrusts.

How Did It Come About? [9]

Formally, a party platform expresses the will of the convention delegates who adopt it. But in both parties, every year, the bulk of the platform has always been written before the delegates come together. In 1972, the Democratic convention adopted an entire preprinted draft platform, amending only two sentences. As we have noted, most delegates did not even read the draft. How, then, was the platform written?

The search for authors leads backward in time, from one group to another, in what seems an infinite regress. The draft platform was adopted by a Platform Committee of 150 members, selected by their state delegations and chaired by Richard E. Neustadt, which met in Washington from June 23 to June 27. The Platform Committee, however, did most of its work through a 15-member Drafting Subcommittee chaired by Kenneth Gibson. The subcommittee, in turn, with only a few days to work, necessarily relied on draft texts prepared by Neustadt's Harvard-oriented staff. But the staff itself was pressed for time and had to deal with the whole range of national issues. Besides composing its own language, the staff incorporated proposals written by a variety of groups—the Democratic Policy

Council, organized labor, civil-rights organizations, and the like—as well as material gathered from testimony in a series of regional hearings held around the country in late May and early June. And the proposals and testimony, in turn, arose from earlier meetings and staff work and from reference to previous documents.

The platform writing, then, involved many contributors and complex lines of influence. The culmination in Washington brought more than a little confusion. Some provisions entered the platform by what can only be termed happenstance. How else is it possible to account for the solemn pledge to end naval shelling of "the tiny, inhabited island of Culebra" no later than June 1, 1975? (P. III:16.) There was at least one outright error: the plank on an independent consumer agency was seriously weakened when the phrase "amicus curiae" was mistakenly underlined instead of crossed out. (P. III:13. See the column by Jack Anderson, *New York Post*, 13 July 1972.) No doubt there were other accidental omissions from the platform, in addition to mistaken inclusions and idiosyncratic language that slipped in during the five hectic days.

Despite this complexity and confusion, certain patterns of action and influence are apparent. First, as we have indicated, the five days of Platform Committee hearings in Washington formed the site where the platform was actually composed. In Washington, the staff work, delegates' ideas, group proposals, and candidates' suggestions were all brought together and synthesized. Second, the major participants in the creation of the platform can be divided into two types, those who participated directly and those whose desires or anticipated reactions were taken into account in the construction of the platform.

Direct participants included what might be called the "policy subculture" of the Democratic party, which we will describe below; organizations and groups allied with (or on speaking terms with) the party; members of the Platform Committee—particularly McGovern delegates on the Drafting Subcommittee and on "task forces"; candidate organizations—chiefly McGovern's; and the Platform Committee staff. To a far lesser extent, they included members of the public, through the

Innovation and Compromise

open platform hearings, and regular convention delegates, through debate and amendment on the convention floor.

But in an ultimate sense the indirect influences were the more important of the two. The full convention had the power to ratify or reject any draft platform, so the reactions of all the convention delegates had to be anticipated at every turn. Similarly, the American public would presumably pass judgment on the document at some point, at least to the extent of punishing truly unpopular stands by withholding votes from the Democratic party: the public's reactions, too, had to be anticipated. While the precise language and detail of the platform were supplied by direct participants, its general thrust undoubtedly resulted from an interplay of the desires of convention delegates (most of whom were, of course, pro-McGovern) and those of the general public, with McGovern's organization mediating the interplay and exercising a gentle veto power. In this interplay, and in the minds of many of the actors, the principal conflict was between advocating "good policies" and winning votes.

In one sense, the writing of the platform began more than a year before the Platform Committee was selected, when the Democratic Policy Council began to hold hearings in January 1971. The Policy Council, chaired by Hubert Humphrey with Edmund Muskie and Lawrence O'Brien as vice-chairmen, was constituted by the 1968 convention. Its six committees and sixteen planning groups, each devoted to a policy area ("Freedom of Information," "Problems of the Elderly," "The Urban Crisis"), held more than twenty hearings during 1971 and early 1972, at which they received testimony from experts and political leaders. Each committee summarized its testimony and platform recommendations in a report; the reports were compiled in a printed booklet, *Alternatives '72*, which was presented to the Platform Committee in May 1972.

Alternatives '72 was an impressive publication. It was much longer and more detailed than the platform itself—184 pages of text. It was less partisan and more thoughtful than the platform, presenting reasons for recommendations and occasionally acknowledging that the Nixon administration was doing things right. Its recommendations were quite specific, often referring to legislation by calendar number, and often specifying dollar amounts of appropriations.

The committee chairmen and contributors included numerous Democratic mayors, governors, and senators, mostly from the liberal wing of the party—Humphrey, Eagleton, McGovern, Gilligan, Bumpers, Maier, Harriman, Stokes; many present and former executive officials—Wilbur Cohen, Ramsay Clark, Nicholas Katzenbach, Roswell Gilpatrick, Newton Minow; and many distinguished academicians—Gardner Ackley, Walter Heller, Richard Falk, Edwin Reischauer, and Stanley Surrey, among others.

The roster of participants in the Democratic Policy Council, in fact, reads like a *Who's Who* of Democratic policy making. It included many men who move in and out of government, serving or advising when the Democrats are in power, testifying before congressional committees, working on Presidential commissions. For them, the Policy Council and the platform are but one arena in which they try to influence policy making. Collectively, they can be termed the *policy subculture* of the Democratic party, and it is this group that provides the party with many of its new ideas and much of its expertise.

How much, then, of the Policy Council's product found its way into the platform? The answer is that much of it, perhaps half the substance of *Alternatives '72*, was eventually included. Occasionally its precise language reached the platform intact. The careful phraseology on busing, which approved of "transportation of students" as "another tool" that must be available to accomplish school desegregation (p. V:4), was taken from *Alternatives '72* (p. 34), as were the references to "walled compounds" in housing segregation (p. 108), and a few other phrases. For the most part, however, the platform closely followed recommendations of *Alternatives '72*, but put them in different language. The booklet supplied both new ideas and considerable continuity with the past.

Some differences between the two documents were notable; the platform took a much harder line on drugs (pp. VI:5–6), ignoring the Policy Council's careful distinctions among marijuana, heroin, and alcohol and omitting the extensive sections on treatment and rehabilitation (p. 17). In foreign affairs, the platform went much farther in favor of disengagement from

Innovation and Compromise 95

Vietnam, decreases in military aid, and support for the Third World; *Alternatives '72* suggestions on these matters were rather diffuse and carried the aura of John Kennedy activism (pp. 138–40, 146–47, 149).

In general the platform was more brief and less specific; it almost always omitted dollar figures, and it toned down controversial proposals to be more pleasing to public opinion. On balance, however, *Alternatives '72* was a major input into the platform that was used extensively by the Platform Committee staff and members alike (each of whom had a copy) as a comprehensive guide and frame of reference. For several busy staff members it provided not only a starting point, but much of the substance of their drafts, which became in turn the basis for the Platform Committee's work.

A second major set of inputs came from organized groups. The Platform Committee, in fact, was deluged with written statements from the elderly, the Gay Activist Alliance, organized labor, women's liberation, Common Cause, the United Farm Workers, and many others. These statements, like *Alternatives '72*, were sometimes cut, pasted, edited, and used by platform drafters.

Organized labor did not (to George Meany's dismay) play its customary powerful role at the 1972 convention. The Platform Committee included few identifiable labor representatives, and the most prominent of those, I. W. Abel, did not participate in its deliberations. Labor did submit a long booklet of *AFL–CIO Platform Proposals,* and most of it corresponded fairly closely with the platform. This happened not because labor's proposals were directly incorporated—the language was almost always different—but because on these matters there was close congruence of goals among everyone involved in platform writing; practically all favored social welfare, taxation, and spending policies that would benefit the working man. As one might expect, the Platform Committee was most attentive to labor's desires in matters directly affecting labor, such as labor-management relations and workmen's compensation.

In areas of conflicting aims, labor's voice did not always prevail. The most striking example is on foreign policy. On Vietnam, the AFL–CIO condemned communist "aggression," and complained about North Vietnamese treatment of prisoners of war; it called for efforts by the United Nations and major communist nations to end the war, without including a word favoring U.S. withdrawal. Labor also criticized trade with the USSR and Nixon's "television spectacular" in China (p. 44). The platform, of course, took an "immediate withdrawal" stand on Vietnam, but its rather grudging approval of improved relations with China and the USSR may have been moderated by labor opposition. The platform went far beyond labor's proposals on the new political groups—women, young people, Indians, and Chicanos. The new issues, which were associated with the McGovern movement—abortion, amnesty, homosexuality—whether alluded to in the platform or merely found in its penumbra of minority reports, seemed to enrage labor leaders.

Even though the platform satisfied all of labor's traditional bread-and-butter demands, and even though it took a moderate position (or none at all) on most of the new issues, many labor leaders took it as an affront. It symbolized the partial displacement of organized labor by new forces in the Democratic party. In this respect the platform (and indeed the convention as a whole) failed to perform its integrative function, and much of the labor movement sat out the November election or worked for Nixon.

The contributions of other groups are not easy to delineate because all their proposals were stirred together in the confusion of the Washington meetings, and there were broad areas of agreement among them. Common Cause, however, shrewdly focused its effort on a few "good government" proposals about electoral and congressional reform. It submitted a handsome glossy pamphlet with suggestions for platform language in large, boldface type, and it had at least one quietly effective worker inside the Platform Committee. The Common Cause proposals on public financing of campaigns, universal voter registration, abolition of the electoral college, and "open meetings" legislation, were inserted in the platform virtually word for word; only the proposal to abolish the seniority system was watered down, presumably in order to appease congressional leaders who were already nervous about McGovern. Similarly, the United Farm Workers' proposals were adopted wholesale, though some inflammatory language was deleted. (The bulk of them were put in the labor section rather than in the one on agriculture, for fear of disturbing farmers.)

The New Democratic Coalition put out a pamphlet, *Platform 1972*, that was used extensively and effectively by liberal members of the Platform Committee in their "task force" revolt against the Drafting Subcommittee. The colorful (pink or yellow) mimeographed handouts of the Gay Activist Alliance provoked debate, but not inclusion. Material supplied by groups of the elderly, people engaged in foreign trade, a conference on children, and the like scored occasional successes.

The influence of Platform Committee members was, in keeping with the spirit of the "new politics," surprisingly great; apparently far greater than in previous years. Neustadt worked on the natural assumption that his staff would do most of the writing, in consultation with the leading Presidential candidates, and that the committee would ratify it. The staff went ahead and prepared drafts for the Washington sessions. On the first day in Washington, Neustadt was elected permanent chairman and moved that the 150-member committee select a more manageable 15-person Drafting Subcommittee. When this procedure was adopted (and an alternative proposal for a more inclusive set of subcommittees was defeated), Neustadt proposed a slate of 15 members for the subcommittee, chosen after consultation with the staffs of the Presidential candidates. The slate was carefully balanced in terms of candidate commitments, with numbers in proportion to delegate strength. Its members were generally mature and "responsible"—that is, fairly amenable to the suggestions of their candidates. The Drafting Subcommittee proceeded to go into private session with candidates' representatives and to debate and polish staff drafts of the platform, while the other 135 Platform Committee members had the task of listening to public testimony over the weekend.

This procedure was entirely in accord with the O'Hara Commission reform rules, but it ran against the mood of the Platform Committee. The committee, like the convention as a whole, seemed full of enthusiastic amateurs; less than one-third of its members had had previous platform experience. The membership also included more women (44 percent), non-whites, and young people than before. These stalwarts of the new politics resented exclusion from the business of platform writing: one member plaintively asked, "Why did we come here, anyhow?" They particularly objected to the implication that a docile drafting subcommittee, acting in their name, was supposed to sit back and ratify staff drafts and candidate suggestions. How did this square with the reform rules and the concept of "participatory democracy"? Their mood was not improved by an afternoon of dull testimony.

In the evening session that first Friday, the Platform Committee members broke into open revolt. One young delegate compained about staff drafts: "Now as a member of this committee, I want to see those drafts if they are going to be used in the platform . . . Why can't I see those drafts? . . ." Neustadt did his best to calm the storm, but the winds were heavy. (An irony of the situation was that only lack of money had thwarted Neustadt's plans to reproduce and distribute drafts as they were prepared.) Nor did it help that Kenneth Gibson, chairman of the Drafting Subcommittee, soothingly remarked, "You don't want to see it anyway . . . It's not so interesting . . . We didn't want to bore you."

While Neustadt consulted with his staff and the Drafting Subcommittee, the young delegate angrily asked, "What are we supposed to do for the next three days while the subcommittee is writing the platform? . . . Can we come to the meetings? Why not? . . . Why are we here?" Other delegates joined in with complaints about exclusion, unrepresented views, closed doors, and secret deals. Anna Chavez won great sympathy with the point that there were no Chicanos on the Drafting Subcommittee, although they made up 15 percent of the Democratic vote in California.

A substantive catalyst of the revolt was the draft section on "Rights, Power, and Social Justice," which was one of the first released. It had been deliberately written in vague generalities; in particular, it made no mention of specific minority groups. The staff's feeling was that once you start a list, where do you stop—with Poles and Lithuanians? But many McGovern delegates and others were eager to mention the groups they considered most powerless and oppressed: the Indians, Puerto Ricans, and Chicanos.

Inexorably, the revolt prevailed. One member of the Drafting Subcommittee resigned so that Anna Chavez could join. Neustadt announced that a few copies of staff drafts would be made available (although few read them; perhaps Gibson's assessment was right), and the full committee set up "task forces" covering each of the eight major issue areas of the platform. It was agreed that those members of the task force whose plank was being discussed in the Drafting Subcommittee could attend the subcommittee meetings.

In subsequent drafting, there was feverish interaction between task forces and the Drafting Subcommittee; the subcommittee frequently had to rewrite its drafts out of fear of defeat in the full 150-member committee. The concrete alternative drafts prepared by some of the task forces (on minorities, agriculture, and government openness, for example) had considerable influence. In addition, the final draft was heavily amended in the full Platform Committee. It was the first time in memory that a national party platform had been written through participatory democracy.

The upshot of all this was that the content of the platform substantially reflected the views of Platform Committee members who came from the new McGovern forces in the Democratic party. This was particularly true of foreign policy, about which committee member Ed Epps of California came armed with many specific proposals; and it was true of the section on "The People and the Government" as well. In the platform section on "Rights, Power, and Social Justice," the members succeeded in changing the bland original draft to specifically mention Indians, Puerto Ricans, and Spanish-speaking Americans as groups that should be brought into the decision-making process. The whole tenor of this plank was different from the original draft. In other words, it was precisely in those areas where the platform was most innovative that the McGovern delegates had their voice.

Some members of the platform committee staff later concluded that the rebellion had been "wonderful": it gave the delegates something harmless to explode about, and removed partisanship from the deliberations; with the press largely absent there was not even any embarrassing publicity. Still, participatory democracy almost went too far for the taste of

McGovern's organization. Monday evening, the fourth day in Washington, when the full committee voted on the work of the Drafting Subcommittee, there were countless amendments from the floor and heated debate. On abortion and homosexuality, the committee came close to adopting planks that might have cost votes in November. Shirley MacLaine's proposal, that a woman's reproductive life was "a matter between her and her doctor," carried by a show of hands, but was subsequently defeated by a roll call vote of 59 to 41; the gay liberation plank for protection of homosexuals in job opportunities and from harassment and arrest was defeated, 54 to 34. In both cases, the hearts of most McGovern delegates were with the proposals, but McGovern's organization made its opposition clear, and enough of his backers voted against the amendments out of fear of alienating Catholics and other voters.

The Platform Committee staff, then, had far less control over proceedings than had been expected. Yet staff members, under Philip Zeidman, Lewis Kaden, and Walter Slocombe, pulled together the suggestions of groups, candidates, and delegates, and wrote substantial platform drafts. The committee was in the strategic position of having more time to work (before the Washington meetings) and more information than anyone else, and of providing the drafts from which work proceeded and which—at least—controlled the agenda and the format. Despite the harrowing experiences with Platform Committee task forces and floor amendments, much of their work survived in the platform.

The aims of the staff were several: to write a platform that contained some innovative and workable policy ideas that they believed in, to appeal to the committee members and delegates who would pass on the platform, to give symbolic recognition to important groups within the Democratic coalition, and to avoid offending voters in the general election. Most important, however, as Neustadt later stated, they wanted to avoid sparring among candidates, and to produce a platform that was acceptable to the Presidential nominee. When, after the California primary, it appeared that the nominee would be McGovern, this meant a liberal platform close in tone to McGovern's previous positions, but very unspecific. Neustadt wanted to leave McGovern room, if he wished, to pull back from his earlier specific stands. Had the nominee been Humphrey, the staff would have sought a platform more liberal than Humphrey's position in tone, but not in substance.

The candidate organizations themselves (predominantly, of course, McGovern's organization) played a central part in the proceedings—not so much in writing platform language as in monitoring it, modifying it, and exercising occasional veto power. In one sense the goals of the major candidates were virtually identical: to dampen the fire of the most liberal members a bit and create a platform that was liberal but not too far to the left of the voters. Muskie, speaking to the committee, advised the drafting of a "moderate" platform. Humphrey's statement warned (with less than perfect tact) against falling "into the hands of any narrow, ideological elite"; the party, in his words, should appeal to the "average American family" (*New York Times*, 25 June 1972). McGovern's representative, Ted Van Dyk, said, "We hope to see a platform that will be liberal, unite the party, and defeat President Nixon in November" (*New York Times*, 24 June 1972).

This coincidence of aims meant that the candidates' staffs and supporters did not seriously conflict in the committee. This was in great contrast to the bitter fighting in the Credentials Committee, where the Presidential nomination itself seemed to be at stake. In the Platform Committee the Humphrey forces sponsored only two minority reports; one an innocuous introduction claiming that past Democratic goals had been "noble" ones (p. MR:2), and the other a proposal for a moratorium on busing for school integration (p. MR:11). Both were easily defeated on the convention floor. The Jackson forces additionally proposed language strengthening the Israel plank (p. MR:13), which was endorsed by McGovern and was accepted, and weakening the Vietnam plank to call for negotiations and mutual withdrawal (p. MR:12), which was overwhelmingly defeated in the convention. For the most part, however, the major candidates would have been content to run on a platform with about the same language on most issues.

Governor Wallace pursued different goals—he wanted the platform to reflect his opposition to crime and disorder, to busing, to federal bureaucracy and spending, to "soft" foreign policy, and to tax exemptions for foundations. Wallace's few members on the Platform Committee were of course hopelessly outnumbered. Yet Wallace represented a significant proportion of the public, and his presence was felt. One of Neustadt's staff men spent a long evening with a Wallace representative working out language on crime and justice; some Wallace rhetoric found its way into this section of the platform, to the outrage of the legal scholar who wrote the original draft. McGovern's staff people (aided by the mediation of a Muskie delegate) also substantially toned down their original pro-busing language in hope of winning Wallace's acceptance and defusing the issue. A near-agreement collapsed, however, perhaps because of the context of overwhelming Wallace defeats on most all other issues, or simply because Wallace wanted a chance to take his hottest issue to the convention floor and national television. Consequently, the Wallace delegates wrote almost an entire alternative platform into minority reports, which were all easily defeated on the convention floor, along with some "unofficial" Wallace proposals submitted by an irrepressible delegate from Florida, Norman Bie.

In the committee itself, the Wallace members tended to be somewhat ignored and isolated, but acrimony was avoided. On the last day in Washington, Mrs. Annie Gunter of Alabama lavishly praised Mayor Kenneth Gibson of Newark, a black McGovern supporter, and pinned a Wallace button on him.

McGovern, along with his staff, deliberately played an unobtrusive role in Washington, since the chief conflict was the awkward one between his desire for a vague and moderate platform—on the theory that a platform "can't help, but could certainly hurt"—and some of his supporters' desires for an unrestrainedly liberal one. McGovern himself, unlike other candidates, did not make an appearance before the committee. There was no need to inflame feelings or disappoint the ardent; he could work behind the scenes and assume that the votes were there when needed.

Despite the surprises and close calls, McGovern was quite successful in monitoring the drafting and in guarding against extreme platform positions. Ted Van Dyk carefully shepherded the drafting process, working with the Drafting Subcommittee throughout its labors and avoiding language that might be construed as needlessly controversial. Meanwhile certain key McGovern committee members—particularly Gibson—helped to keep the Drafting Subcommittee in line and soothe upset members of the full committee. McGovern was probably sincerely pleased when he called the draft platform a "splendid document," "forward looking," and one that would appeal to the "new center" of the political spectrum (*New York Times*, 28 June 1972).

There had been a novel effort to ensure citizen participation in the framing of the platform. The Platform Committee had held twelve regional hearings around the country, beginning May 30, and the public was invited to testify. Thousands of pages of testimony were taken—often colorful, occasionally bizarre. People spoke about racism in South Africa, homosexual rights, Northern Irish Catholics, aid for the Arabs, tax reform, American Indians, and consumer cooperatives. (See, for example, the *New York Times*, 14 June 1972.) The dominant tone was one of discontent and cynicism; at the very least, therefore, the hearings helped convey the impression that America was sick of Republican leadership. In addition, the people gained a sense of contributing to and participating in the writing of the platform; the hearings helped to give it the aura of a genuinely popular document.

The staff tried to take this public input seriously and prepared an elaborately indexed library of testimony for the use of the Drafting Subcommittee. Realistically, however, no one could digest the thousands of pages of position papers and transcripts in the few weeks available to the staff, let alone the few days allotted to the Drafting Subcommittee. The library was largely ignored. Only a few suggestions gathered during the hearings found their way into the platform. These were ideas or phrases that caught the fancy of the committee staff and were preserved.

The convention as a whole, as we have said, altered only two sentences in the entire draft platform; it added that the United States should maintain military forces ". . . in Europe and at sea in the Mediterranean ample to deter the Soviet Union from putting unbearable pressure on Israel" (p. MR:13), and it inserted the sentence, "In addition, we support allocation of federal surplus lands to American Indians on a first priority basis" (p. MR:9). This was just as McGovern had wished. The first amendment was proposed by Senator Jackson and endorsed by McGovern; the second was declared a "free vote" by the McGovern organization.

All other minority reports—including Senator Harris's redistributive tax reform (which would treat all income equally, abolishing, for example, preferential treatment of capital gains and municipal bonds), the National Welfare Rights Organization's $6,500 income plan, the sexual reproduction plank, and Humphrey's and Jackson's proposals on busing and Vietnam, and Wallace's alternative platform—were opposed by McGovern. After long and spirited debates, all were defeated. Only the tax reform plan came close to passage; it was declared defeated on a voice vote, but many observers thought the vote went in favor of the plan.

The fact that the delegates did not substantially change the platform, however, certainly does not mean that they had no influence on its content. They held the ultimate power of adoption or rejection, and they exerted profound influence through their representation on the Platform Committee and through others' anticipations of their reactions. Indeed, the McGovern insurgents were responsible for much of the innovative thrust of the platform. The defeat of the minority reports, however, was also a victory for Senator McGovern and his organization—a victory, in no small measure, over certain inclinations of his own delegates.

The convention delegates had plenty of thoughts about what should be in the platform; when they were interviewed, nearly all the Wallace delegates and a large majority of McGovern supporters mentioned specific planks. (See Table 3.)

When we asked delegates what they would like to see in the platform, or what they would not like to see, some party regulars replied that they didn't really care. "Oh, the standard inclusions of a typical Democratic platform," said one Connecticut leader; only when pressed did he cite Social Security, education, and national health insurance. Another said that the Democratic party should "do things for people, within their ability to pay, without taking away their pride and even depriving them of shame. . . ." Others, as we have seen, sim-

TABLE 3. Percentages of Delegates Who Mentioned Specific Platform Topics, by Candidate Commitment *

Number of topics mentioned	CANDIDATE COMMITMENT		
	McGovern	Wallace	Regulars
0	22% (28)	4% (1)	40% (18)
1	20 (25)	43 (10)	27 (12)
2	31 (39)	22 (5)	22 (10)
3	14 (18)	22 (5)	4 (2)
4 or more	13 (16)	9 (2)	7 (3)
	100 (126)	100 (23)	100 (45)

* The delegates were asked what they wanted excluded from or included in the platform. "Regular" candidates are Muskie, Humphrey, and Jackson. The values are significant at $p = .01$ by the chi-square test. The figures within parentheses are the numbers of cases upon which the percentages are based.

ply said the platform was irrelevant and offered few or no thoughts about it. "Heck, I really don't know now. That amnesty is really a big thing in Missouri. . . ."

Some party regulars spoke out against the new directions the party was taking, sometimes in bitterly emotional terms. Several said the Democrats should not be "spokesmen for Hanoi" who urge North Vietnam not to accept Nixon's peace terms; they opposed amnesty, legalization of marijuana, and (sometimes in unprintable language) homosexual rights.

For most of the new issue-oriented delegates, however, the platform was of greater importance, and they wanted it to be progressive, especially on the new issues. A black woman, one of few delegates who had read the draft platform, said it was "pretty fair," but that more could be added to "help the poor, little people, the underrepresented." Others poured forth specific suggestions, often focusing on the minority reports: a Jewish radical from New York "strenuously" opposed the pro-Israel amendment; he favored the Harris tax-reform proposal, and the gay-rights amendment—he was "very upset" at a derogatory antihomosexual speech; and he was "very, very happy about the Indians . . . that was the happiest thing about the whole convention, except McGovern's nomination."

A Chicano from the anti-Daley "Chicago 59" emphasized bilingual education and the $6,500 income proposal. A black legislator from Wisconsin liked the language about Africa and wanted a strong proabortion stand, legalization of *all* drugs, elimination of *all* prisons. An Iowa farmer thought the draft platform was very, very good on agriculture and the war; he especially favored measures to stop migration to the cities. A New Yorker rattled off his opposition to Wallace planks and his support for women's rights, gay liberation, the Harris tax reform, stronger gun control, and welfare rights. McGovern delegates, of course, were not the only issue-oriented ones; a pro-Wallace woman from Michigan spoke up in well-informed detail for Wallace's proposals on busing, amnesty, review of federal judges, abortion, and gun control.

As these examples suggest, the concerns of the delegates centered on new issues of life style, the war, and income distribution. In our interviews they emphasized abortion most of all, followed by Vietnam, busing, tax reform, and guaranteed income. Mentions of traditional Democratic concerns such as medical care or aid to education were rare. (See Table 4.) Wallace delegates seemed single-mindedly concerned with busing—83 percent volunteered that they favored an antibusing

TABLE 4. Percentages of Delegates Who Mentioned Specific Platform Topics, by Topic *

Abortion (sexual reproduction)	33%
Vietnam withdrawal	28
Busing for integration	24
Harris tax reform	19
Guaranteed income	19
Gay liberation (homosexual rights)	12
Amnesty for Vietnam resisters	8
Military aid for Israel	7
Legalization of drugs	6
Defense budget cuts	5
Law and order	4
Indian land and rights	3
Lettuce boycott	1

* The delegates were asked what they wanted excluded from or included in the platform.

plank, and many mentioned nothing else. McGovern delegates frequently cited the abortion issue (42 percent), Vietnam (33 percent), guaranteed income (24 percent), and tax reform (21 percent).

Without question the sentiments of the delegates were quite liberal, probably much more so than those of the average American. A CBS poll showed that about 70 percent of the delegates supported busing for school integration, at least where busing was "the only available tool"; 71 percent favored some sort of Vietnam amnesty (about half of those insisted on some form of alternative national service); and 64 percent favored a guaranteed annual income for all people (*Miami Herald,* 8 July 1972).

In our interviews, those who mentioned platform issues—particularly the McGovern delegates—were especially liberal: of those taking a stand on the Harris tax-reform proposal, 91 percent supported it; 87 percent supported Vietnam withdrawal; and 79 percent favored a guaranteed income. Only on abortion and gay liberation were options about evenly (and intensely) divided, and 77 percent of the comments on busing (mostly from Wallace supporters) opposed the issue. In every case, the comments of McGovern delegates were more liberal than those of others.[10]

The CBS poll and our interviews suggest that a majority of delegates, at least in their personal opinions, favored some of the positions taken in "minority" planks. Almost certainly this was true of tax reform and the $6,500 guaranteed income; quite possibly it applied to abortion as well. Yet many who believed in these policies voted against the inclusion of them in the platform, and, thus, all three were defeated. How could this come about?

An important but partial answer is that "the word came down" from McGovern, and most of his delegates complied out of loyalty to him. The word was spread in a low-key fashion with a certain delicacy; McGovern's floor managers had a brief set of written instructions that expressed sympathy for each of these proposals, but that indicated opposition. In each of these three cases, the instructions said "Position: Against, although those who feel particularly strongly in behalf of the minority plank should feel free to vote accordingly."

(On the Wallace and most other minority reports, it said flatly, "Position: Against.") Despite a few painful incidents of pressure (more than one woman was seen to cry when browbeaten by male delegates to vote against the abortion plank), most voting suggestions were conveyed in friendly and deferential fashion, to amenable delegates, and few said they had been subjected to "arm twisting."

The McGovern instruction sheet summarized its position as follows: "We strongly support the majority plank. . . . Our objective: to support in general the majority planks, without divisive or rancorous debate." This objective was met; the debates on potentially embarrassing issues like abortion and homosexuality were scheduled for early morning hours when the television audience was minimal.

The reasoning that led McGovern to oppose these minority reports is simple enough—he wanted to win in November. In accord with Downsian theories of campaigning, McGovern wanted to take stands that would be acceptable to as many Americans as possible; that is, moderate or middle-of-the-road stands. His campaign had in fact followed a course consistent with a two-stage, dynamic theory of campaigning: first appealing to and activating young campaign workers; then, as he approached victory for the nomination, shifting closer to the middle ground to appeal to average voters.

Throughout 1971 McGovern had toured the college campuses, enlisting recruits for his "new politics" campaign. In those appearances, he allowed students to believe (while generally using careful language) that he agreed with them, that he wanted to legalize marijuana, to get out of Vietnam at once, to declare an amnesty for draft dodgers and deserters, and to liberalize abortion laws. At that time he was the only national political figure taking such stands. The young signed aboard the campaign, organized key primary states, canvassed door-to-door, packed local caucuses, and attended state conventions. Coming from nowhere in the public opinion polls—preferred by fewer than 5 percent of Democrats at the beginning of 1972—McGovern and his workers achieved their astonishing upset, and won the Democratic nomination.

As he prospered in the primaries, McGovern first tried to broaden his appeal beyond Vietnam and the student issues.

He began talking about economic questions, still maintaining his position as the bold, specific candidate of the left. Soon, however, he began to move toward the center. His $1,000 income-grant proposal became merely an "example" of possible welfare reform; while he continued to favor tax reform, his *Wall Street Journal* advertisement (Pacific Coast edition, 24 May 1972) denied any explicit commitment to the taxing of capital gains; he asserted that abortion was a "local issue" on which he would take no stand; and he rejected the idea of legalizing marijuana. All this was done artfully while loudly denying any change. He was not moving to the center, McGovern said; a "new center" was coming to him. The platform, progressive but mild, completed his shift.

Whether McGovern, with a reputation for candor and integrity, was bothered by this fudging is not clear. Certainly he could point out that important differences remained between himself and Nixon on Vietnam, the defense budget, and income distribution. As a pragmatic politician he could plead necessity: What good would bold policy stands do if he were not elected to carry them out? Why obscure the central issues of the campaign with emotional matters of "style" like marijuana and abortion? Why jeopardize the chances of victory? In any event, he could argue that his precise language had been largely consistent; let the audiences answer for any changes in nuance they imagined. Still, McGovern may have felt some personal unease as he dealt with the politician's classic dilemma.

Personal unease aside, the dilemma of how to win over the middle American without losing the young legions involved a difficult operation. Its hazards were revealed in the Platform Committee revolt by the task forces and in the debate at Miami Beach over the minority reports. Many McGovern delegates were disappointed by the sellout of women's rights and tax reform; a handful vowed to drop out of the campaign. But the problem was most sharply underlined on the crucial issue of Vietnam, the very core of McGovern's early campaign. The average American, though he wanted the war over and American boys home, seemed indifferent to the blasting and burning of the Vietnamese; but the moral outrage of many young people over the killing of Asians had provided much of the energy of the campaign. When, therefore, McGovern indicated to a group of POW wives in Miami Beach that he would keep some residual forces in Thailand until the POWs were returned, he set off an explosion of anger and disappointment. It did not matter that McGovern was technically consistent with his pledge to get entirely out of *Indochina* (Thailand is not in Indochina)—the McGovern delegates wanted all U.S. forces out of Southeast Asia, *now!* The outcry among delegates and a noisy demonstration by Zippies were so strong that McGovern made his strongest Vietnam statement to that time. Vietnam, at least, was sacred.

In any event, McGovern's push for a moderate platform caused the major conflicts of platform writing, which were the conflicts with his own delegates. McGovern's will and efforts played a big part in the final compromise between what his delegates thought was right, and what the people wanted to hear.

But the delegates themselves were not immune to Downsian logic; in the end, they voted down the liberal minority reports, not just out of obedience to McGovern, but because they, too, were thinking about what would be "effective," what would help gain victory in November. Most of the delegates we interviewed showed some awareness of the conflict between ideological purity and political effectiveness, and most showed at least some willingness to compromise.

A few insisted on purity: "You've gotta say what the country needs," even if it costs votes. "I want those things in, because I *believe* in them . . . it's possible we could lose votes . . . but it's a matter of principle." "Look, I mean if you *believe* something, put it in; don't lie." Almost two-fifths of those explaining their platform stands relied exclusively on ideological correctness.

Many favored some compromise. A woman from Chicago expressed anguish about the abortion issue, on which she personally favored the minority report: "It was a hard decision. It didn't belong in a platform . . . I wanted a platform that could elect a Democratic President." A McGovern leader commented that "You have to strike a balance . . . progressive, yet politically useful." Even a firebreathing New Yorker was responsive to the dilemma in his own way: "If a plank is too far off the mainstream, you lose votes, you have to go back . . . For example, you can't advocate compulsory abortion. The minority plank was just *voluntary*. The gay plank was voluntary; nobody is going to *force* people to be gay. It was *very moderate*." So begins political compromise.

Indeed, we found that, in apparent contradiction to the conventional wisdom, McGovern delegates did not tend to be ideological purists about the platform any more than did backers of the regular candidates. Only the Wallace delegates tended to completely ignore the matter of winning votes; as many McGovernites as regulars cited this function of the platform as one of their concerns. (See Table 5.)

TABLE 5. Percentages of Delegates with Various Goals for Platform, by Candidate Commitment

Goal for platform	CANDIDATE COMMITMENT			
	McGovern	Wallace	Regulars	Total
Winning votes	24% (18)	0% (0)	24% (7)	21% (25)
Ideological purity	41 (31)	58 (7)	48 (14)	44 (52)
Both of the above	24 (18)	0 (0)	21 (6)	21 (24)
Other	12 (9)	42 (5)	7 (2)	14 (16)
	100 (76)	100 (12)	100 (29)	100 (117)

* Entries are based on delegates' explanations of why they wanted particular planks (or none) excluded from or included in the platform. The 40 percent who did not answer this question are excluded from the analysis, and those predominantly concerned with winning or correctness are combined with those who were exclusively concerned with these effects. "Regular" candidates are Muskie, Humphrey, and Jackson. The values are significant at $p < .10$.

For many of the new McGovern delegates, the platform fights forced the first taste of compromise. They were bringing an infusion of new ideas, new people, and revitalization into the Democratic party. Many would undoubtedly stay with the party, just as a large group of McCarthy workers from 1968 became McGovern delegates in 1972. But those who stayed on would face repeated choices between what was right and what would sell, painful conflicts between idealism and pragmatism.

Conclusion: What Did It All Mean?

For the People contained some lively, creative, liberal proposals of a rather specific character. Whether it would foreshadow years of legislation, as did the 1948 Democratic platform, remained to be seen, but it was at least an authentic sign of new forces in the Democratic party. At the same time, it represented compromise as well as innovation. The platform illustrated both Downsian and "responsible party" aspects of party behavior, and showed how parties act as followers as well as leaders of public opinion.

The year 1972 was one of infusion of new ideas and new faces into the Democratic party. The new wave of McGovern delegates cared about issues and about the platform. They wanted an end to the Vietnam involvement, demilitarization of foreign policy, restrictions on big business, redistribution of income. They wanted amnesty, privacy, freedom of sexual activity and life style, open and participatory government. They wanted symbolic recognition and concrete benefits for women, the young, Chicanos, Indians, homosexuals, even prisoners. And most of these desires were written—if in somewhat muted form—into the platform, joining with the more traditional social welfare stands of the Democratic party.

But the making of a platform involves an inevitable conflict between delegates' desires and public opinion. For, as McClosky and others have shown,[11] convention delegates and political activists are not average people; their opinions differ from those of the mass, and many of them enter politics precisely because they want to turn their opinions into policy. Yet delegates also want to win elections and must heed the wishes of the public. Presidential candidates, too, have opinions of their own, but they also want to please delegates and win a nomination, activate workers for the general election, and win votes from the public. In writing a platform, or taking a policy stand of any kind, these conflicting aims must be reconciled.

In 1972, many issue stands of the McGovern movement were perceived—probably correctly—as being far to the left of predominant public opinion. It was believed that the American public had a deep fear of drugs—even marijuana, revulsion at homosexuality, abhorrence of abortion, outrage at the idea of amnesty for Vietnam draft resisters, reluctance to withdraw hastily from Vietnam, lukewarm attitudes toward integration and hostility to busing, anxiety about military budget cuts that might imperil national security, and absolute opposition to welfare or a guaranteed income.[12]

On several of these issues (most notably amnesty, Vietnam, busing, and "income security"), the McGovernites wrote stands into their platform that probably went beyond what the public wanted. But on many issues, with active effort by McGovern's staff and at least the acquiescence of his delegates, they compromised. Planks dealing with abortion, homosexuality, and drug legalization were deleted altogether from the platform. The phrase "guaranteed income" was not mentioned, and the $6,500 income proposal was rejected. Busing ("transportation") was timidly alluded to as "one tool" for school integration. Military budget cuts were advocated only in mild language. The new, issue-oriented forces in the party, in other words, faced up to the politician's dilemma. In making the platform and voting on minority planks, they decided to subordinate some of their beliefs in the name of expediency.

It is not easy to evaluate this decision. On the one hand, we might celebrate the willingness of the McGovern delegates to compromise. Far from being hard-bitten radicals, or rigid ideologues, they engaged in give-and-take. They partook of the essence of politics—they "worked within the system."

Yet there is something poignant about political professionalization. Once compromise begins, it is hard to stop. One policy here, another there, is discarded as "impractical," and eventually the idealistic fire may be lost. As one weather-beaten delegate remarked, "Winners have a way of becoming the Establishment."

Moreover, in this particular setting (and, more pointedly, in the McGovern campaign as a whole) one might argue that too much was compromised. With the hindsight provided by the electoral disaster in November, it is clear that the McGovern movement failed to convince America that it had moved to the political center. Despite appeals to the working man, labor defected from the Democrats; despite the platform's moderation and the rejection of minority planks, Mc-

Govern was still tagged as the "triple A" candidate (for acid, abortion, and amnesty).

Perhaps a two-stage campaign is an impossible dream. Perhaps voters refuse to forget earlier positions and the character of original supporters. (Barry Goldwater's experience is suggested.) If so, a minority movement that captures a party nomination might do better to sail into defeat with banners flying and conduct a deliberately educational campaign. Might it not have been useful to provoke full national discussion of the proper governmental approach to homosexuality and abortion? Couldn't much have been said about guaranteed income, redistributive taxation, the arms race?

Advocates of low-temperature consensus politics would be horrified at the thought, however, and political scientists would point out that it is hard to resist vote-maximizing pressures, and that it may be impossible to carry on rational discourse in an election campaign.

NOTES

1. Anthony Downs, *An Economic Theory of Democracy* (New York: Harper & Row, 1957); Otto A. Davis, Melvin J. Hinich, and Peter C. Ordeshook, "An Expository Development of a Mathematical Model of the Electoral Process," *American Political Science Review*, vol. 64 (June 1970): 426–48.

2. Committee on Political Parties, American Political Science Association, "Toward a More Responsible Two-Party System," *American Political Science Review*, vol. 44, no. 3, pt. 2 (September 1950).

3. Gerald M. Pomper, *Elections in America* (New York: Dodd, Mead, 1968), Chap. 8.

4. For background, see Irwin Ross, *The Loneliest Campaign: the Truman Victory of 1948* (New York: New American Library, 1968). For the texts of this and other platforms, see Kirk H. Porter and Donald B. Johnson, *National Party Platforms, 1840–1964* (Urbana, Ill.: University of Illinois Press, 1966).

5. See Theodore H. White, *The Making of the President 1968* (New York: Atheneum, 1969).

Innovation and Compromise

6. Theodore H. White, *The Making of the President 1960* (New York: Atheneum, 1961).

7. Rexford G. Tugwell, *The Brains Trust* (New York: Viking, 1968).

8. This and succeeding page numbers refer to the printed pamphlet, *For the People,* presented to the 1972 Democratic National Convention as a report of the Platform Committee. Citations to the 1968 platform refer to a similar document, *Toward a More Perfect Union,* Chicago, Illinois, August 27, 1968.

9. For much of the preconvention material in this section I am indebted to Michael Marohn. I am also grateful to Richard Neustadt and Chris Arterton for their comments and suggestions.

10. Although these findings are based on very small numbers and do not individually reach statistical significance, they reveal a highly consistent pattern across a number of issues.

11. Herbert McClosky, Paul J. Hoffman, and Rosemary O'Hara, "Issue Conflict and Consensus Among Party Leaders and Followers," *American Political Science Review,* vol. 54 (June 1960): 406–27.

12. For a discussion of the opinions of Americans on some of these issues (based on earlier data), see Richard M. Scammon and Ben J. Wattenberg, *The Real Majority* (New York: Coward-McCann, 1970).

chapter five

Winners and Losers
The Impact of Power on Purism and Professionalism

. . . .

On Thursday afternoon, the day after McGovern was nominated, Mrs. Reinhart, a Nevada housewife who had made a last minute switch to Jackson after Humphrey dropped out of the race, spoke of the need for reconciliation and party unity:[1] "Party unity is a prerequisite for defeating Nixon and it's also necessary to improve the economic and tax situation . . . Also in order to improve race relations." Despite her frustration at seeing Humphrey defeated, she was able to shift her focus from the issues dividing the party to those which divided Democrats and Republicans. For her, the most important goal was to unify the party to defeat Nixon, and by Thursday evening she was cheering McGovern's acceptance speech and thinking about the things to be done between the convention and election day.

But a more typical response among backers of the losing candidates was that of a Pennsylvania Humphrey supporter, John Capuzzo, who commented to one of our interviewers on Thursday after the nomination of McGovern, "Wednesday night's vote shows that we'll have to sit down and think things out when we get back home. What things?—supporting McGovern and getting him to moderate his positions." While Mrs. Reinhart was cheering McGovern on Thursday evening, many like Capuzzo had packed their bags and left Miami before McGovern's acceptance speech on Thursday.

Both Capuzzo and Reinhart were losers, but both reacted

in different ways, and each exemplified a different view of the function and dynamics of national nominating conventions. For Mrs. Reinhart, McGovern had become the legitimate choice of the convention, while for Capuzzo the differences between McGovern and Humphrey remained unbridgeable.

The winners at the convention displayed, like the losers, different reactions to the reality of McGovern's victory. On Thursday afternoon a young McGovern delegate from California, John Robinson, talked of his reactions: "People have worked very hard for McGovern. The people I know have the very purest attitudes. We knew people who went for Muskie, but we feel a brave antiwar person had to be supported." Robinson, as yet, was unaware of the problems of power—of the need for the support of men like Cappuzo if the announced centrist strategy of McGovern was to be successful.[2] The business of the convention Thursday night was the selection of a Vice-Presidential nominee. Robinson talked of his desire to have the party nominate Senator Gravel of Alaska for Vice-President because of his correct position on all the major issues. Issue correctness was a consuming passion for Robinson.[3]

But not all the winners at the convention were like Robinson. Susan Wriston, another young McGovern delegate interviewed by us Thursday, expressed the same sort of concern with party unity as did the Jackson supporter, Mrs. Reinhart: "What I'd like to see come out of it is a unified party. I don't think that's possible, but things have been done . . . party unity is important to defeat Nixon . . . HHH, Muskie, because it is politically expedient, will support McGovern. Labor is a problem . . . I can't see McGovern making concessions." One might say that Wriston had gone halfway down the road to thinking like a party regular. She recognized the problem and faced it squarely by saying that McGovern could not win without party unity, but then backed off by saying that McGovern ought not to sacrifice his principles. She saw McGovern's former adversaries coming to support him because they would do what was politically expedient, an option she denied to McGovern.[4]

We can think of the four delegates whose views we have described from the interviews of Thursday in terms of their concern with party unity or issue purity and whether they are part of a winning or a losing coalition. (See Table 1.)

TABLE 1. Concerns of Delegates on Thursday Afternoon After McGovern's Nomination

	Party unity or reconciliation	Issue purity of the nominee
Favored McGovern	Wriston	Robinson
Favored losing candidate	Reinhart	Capuzzo

At first glance, it might appear that Robinson and Capuzzo are the issue-oriented delegates and Wriston and Reinhart, the party people. But Capuzzo is a strong Democrat who thinks of himself as representing rank-and-file Democrats in his home district. Wriston, on the other hand, refuses to identify herself with the party, preferring, instead, to think of herself as a strong independent who represents the interests of women and young people. The first concern of this issue-oriented delegate on Thursday afternoon, however, was party unity. Thus we have an anomaly in which an issue-oriented delegate expresses a concern with party, and a party regular, a concern with issues.

Some light may be shed on the problem if we compare the two supporters of losing candidates, Reinhart and Capuzzo. Both are strong Democrats who represent the interests of rank-and-file Democrats from their home districts. And both originally supported Humphrey for the nomination. But differences begin to appear when we look at their attitudes toward issues and groups. Capuzzo, on the one hand, expresses strong support for the interests of labor and, at the same time, a certain coolness toward the interests of blacks, women, and youth. Reinhart, in contrast, is very cool toward the interests of labor and warms toward blacks, women, and youth. The rancor with which Capuzzo spoke seems based, in part, on his perception of the group identifications of McGovern and his celebrated new constituency strategy, which proclaimed reduced dependence upon labor as a basis of support. The difference between Capuzzo's rejection of McGovern and Reinhart's acceptance is, it seems, a simple matter of issue correctness, a disease against which party regulars may not be immunized.

The Effects of Winning and Losing on Political Purism

The themes we have isolated in the responses of the four delegates run through the literature on party organization and participation. The distinction between the issue-oriented (ideologically pure) and the party-oriented delegate has been utilized in a variety of different studies of political participation and, especially in the 1960s, in studies of national nominating conventions. Although the arrival of "purists" as a significant element in nomination politics was noted by Aaron Wildavsky in his commentary on the 1964 Republican convention, their importance was presaged by James Q. Wilson in his book on the emergence of amateur Democratic clubs in three cities in the late 1950s.[5] His analysis revealed a recurring conflict between Democratic regulars and issue-oriented amateurs. For Wilson, the issue orientations of the amateur are connected, not to self or narrow group interest, but to a larger public interest. For the amateur, participation in politics becomes an extension of private morality into the public sector. In his analysis of Goldwater delegates at the 1964 Republican convention, Wildavsky spoke of the distinction between purists and politicians in much the same way as Wilson did for that between amateur and regular Democrats. Wildavsky continued the purist versus professional theme in his study of the 1968 Democratic convention, casting the young McCarthyites in the role of purist and the Humphrey supporters in the role of professional. In a more quantitative study of the same convention, Soule and Clarke developed a measure of purism or, as they called it, amateurism, that separated quite nicely the McCarthy supporters from the Humphrey delegates.[6] It seemed, then, that purism was not the sole property of the right; it could serve to distinguish rightist Goldwater delegates from more centrist Republican party regulars as well as leftist McCarthyites from more centrist professional Democrats.

The McGovern surge in the 1972 primaries and state convention contests for delegates was a continuation of the earlier

McCarthy movement. The same themes of political reform and purism dominated the rhetoric of the McGovern organization. And again, as in 1968, the conflict between the McGovern organization and the regulars—the supporters of Humphrey-Muskie-Jackson—was as much a clash of styles as it was a conflict over policy; the antichrist of the purist was again the traditional party politician or regular. Table 2 draws upon the

TABLE 2. Purist–Professional Orientations

	Purist	Professional
A. Nomination of candidate	Candidate preference is justified in terms of his correct stand on the issues.	Candidate preference is justified in terms of his capacity to unify the party and win elections. Issue preferences are relevant but subordinate.
B. Issue preferences and platforms	Correct issue positions are arrived at in terms of some conception of a public interest or good.	Issue positions are correct if they, in the context of the convention and election, placate losers without alienating followers and, at the same time, offer a chance of winning the general election.
C. Convention decision	Issue differences, which are acknowledged to exist, are resolved through open discussion and debate in which each participant has equal weight. Thus intraparty democracy becomes a strong value and is perceived as a device for discovering the correct issue position.	Issue differences are resolved through bargaining and compromise in which the outcome is determined, to a large extent, by the relative power positions of contending groups. Intraparty democracy is not a strong value.

D. Party orientation	Parties are viewed as devices for expressing correct policy preferences so that voters are offered clear choices.	Party policy positions are accepted as reasonably fixed in the short run and are strongly preferred to those of alternative party. Attention is turned not to the expression of correct policy but to problems of organizational maintenance and mobilization of support at the polls.

studies of Wilson, Wildavsky, and Soule and Clarke to compare the distinguishing features of the purist–professional types. What adds fascination to these opposing role descriptions are the views that the incumbents of each have of the other. For purists, professionals have neither the skills nor the incentive for consciousness raising or ideological clarification; for professionals, purists do not have the patience or the respect for differences in issue positions required for the process of mutual adjustment and bargaining. Because the professional has learned the value of mutual adjustment and concern for party unity from bitter experience, he looks upon the purist as, at best, simple-minded and, at worst, destructive. The purist believes that the politics practiced by the professional are somehow "unclean."

Thus political style has been treated as an enduring characteristic of the person rather than of the particular political situation in which he finds himself. But this may be an oversimplification. It is easy for the party regular to be a professional in a process of mutual adjustment when the center of gravity in the party reflects his issue position. The insurgent purist, on the other hand, worries more about issues precisely because the center of the party is so far removed from his issue preferences. Note the difference between purist and professional in the party orientation category of Table 2. The purist worries about issues, while the professional worries about **organization**.

Other elements of the purist–professional dichotomy lend themselves to the same analysis. The rallying cry of the purists for intraparty democracy is also a request for reduction in the power of the regulars relative to that of insurgents. The reiteration of themes of moral purity is also a device for maintaining incentives for participation where there are no material rewards. Insurgents demand policy-making arenas where rational discussion and open debate predominate; from another perspective this is a demand that skills possessed by a middle-class insurgent group be weighed more heavily in policy making.

If style is partially a response to one's fortunes in the organization, a reversal of roles might be expected as the purists approach positions of leadership responsibility and as the regulars are displaced. Yesterday's regular is tomorrow's purist worried about the issue integrity of a party he no longer owns. And yesterday's purist is today's professional worried about organizational unity, incentives, and winning elections.

Regardless of which perspective we adopt in considering political style, almost all commentators agree that the McGovern and Wallace organizations were far more purist in style than were the Humphrey-Muskie-Jackson delegates. When we look at how the candidate organizations change over the course of the convention, the relevance of the differences between these two perspectives on style becomes apparent. If political style is independent of winning and losing, then we should expect no pronounced changes in orientation among McGovern supporters as they move into positions of leadership in the party. And those who are professionals on Monday should be party professionals on Friday. On the other hand, if political style responds to winning and losing, then we should expect the McGovern forces to become increasingly pragmatic over the course of the convention, and the Humphrey-Muskie-Jackson delegates, increasingly purist. It is to this issue we now turn.

The Stability of Political Style—a Test

To test our notions on political style we developed a measure of the delegates' purist or professional perspectives from our interview data. Each delegate was asked to state what he really wanted to see done at the convention and the reasons for his preference. Using the guidelines in Table 2, we classified each delegate goal in reason (value) in Table 3.

Thus of the 234 delegates interviewed we were able to classify 187 or 80 percent. In all our subsequent discussions of

TABLE 3. Classification of Delegates as Either Purist or Professional

A. Nomination of candidate	If delegate goal was nomination of preferred candidate because his candidate could win in November	= Professional $N = 11$ *
	If delegate goal was nomination of preferred candidate because candidate was correct on the issues, or correctly represented new groups or party reform	= Purist $N = 76$
B. Issue preference and platform	If delegate goal was party unity because of need to win in November, or if delegate goal was issue in platform because it would aid winning in November	= Professional $N = 27$
	If delegate goal was correct issue in platform for any other reason	= Purist $N = 19$
C. Convention decision process	If delegate goal was representation of new groups in convention decision making and party decision making, or party reform	= Purist $N = 26$
D. Party orientation	If delegate goal was nomination of winner to unify party, express traditional issues dividing Republicans and Democrats	= Professional $N = 28$

* N is the number in the sample.

purist versus political perspectives, we shall be using this measure. Of course, the validity of a measure of purism–professionalism would be in doubt if it did not differentiate McGovern supporters from those supporting Humphrey-Jackson-Muskie. Our measure does so quite handsomely in Table 4.

TABLE 4. The Delegates' Purism and Professionalism, by Candidate Preference *

	Purist	Professional	Total
Preference for McGovern	83% (98)	17% (11)	109
Preference for Wallace	65 (11)	35 (6)	17
Preference for HHH, Muskie, or Jackson	45 (22)	55 (27)	49
Total	70%	30%	175

* Candidate preference was assessed by asking each delegate the name of the candidate he most preferred for the nomination regardless of how he had voted or intended to vote. The results are roughly the same as the preconvention vote preference recorded by CBS for each delegate.

But what is even more noteworty is that the level of purism in the McGovern group far outstrips that of the Wallacites, the other important candidate group driven by strong issue orientation. Not only does the McGovern organization display a high level of purism but it has all the other characteristics associated with purism. As Table 5 shows, the rank-and-file McGovern delegates tend to be weak party identifiers with little prior convention experience. Their level of amauteurism —a consequence in part of the reform rules—is exceeded only by that of the Wallace organization. In subsequent analyses we will restrict our attention to McGovern delegates and supporters of Humphrey, Muskie, or Jackson. Our principal concern in this section revolves around the relationship between the McGovern organization and the Democratic regulars. The relationship of the Wallacites to the main axis of the convention will be discussed in a later part of our study.

As the attentive reader might expect, there is a close rela-

TABLE 5. Delegates' Involvement in Party, by Candidate Preference *

	Amateur	Identification only	Identification and prior experience
Preference for Wallace	52% (12)	35% (8)	13% (30)
Preference for McGovern	43 (54)	47 (39)	10 (13)
Preference for HHH, Muskie, or Jackson	17 (10)	53 (31)	29 (17)

* *Amateurs* are either weak or nonparty identifiers with no prior convention experience; *identification only* are those with strong party identification and no prior convention experience; *identification and prior convention experience* are those with strong party identification and prior convention experience.

tionship between purism and the nature and extent of party involvement. Amateurs are more than twice as likely as regulars to adopt what we have labeled a purist political style in thinking about convention events.[7] In addition, the purists tend to be younger, to perceive the platform as a matter of some importance, and to think of themselves as representing groups in a national constituency—blacks, women, and youth. The professionals, on the other hand, are less impressed with the importance of the party platform, tend more to think of themselves as representing the rank-and-file Democrats of their home district or state, and are significantly older than the purists. The findings are strikingly similar to those of Soule and Clarke in their study of 1968 Humphrey and McCarthy delegates.[8]

But when we turn to the results on change over the course of the convention, some interesting differences begin to emerge. As Figure 1 illustrates, the hypothesis that McGovern delegates would grow increasingly pragmatic as their organization assumed a position of leadership in the convention was not confirmed. The delegates, it seems, were willing to accept the discipline imposed upon them for the sake of a McGovern victory in the convention, but they were unwilling to follow

FIGURE 1.

Purist Orientation Among McGovern and Non-McGovern Delegates

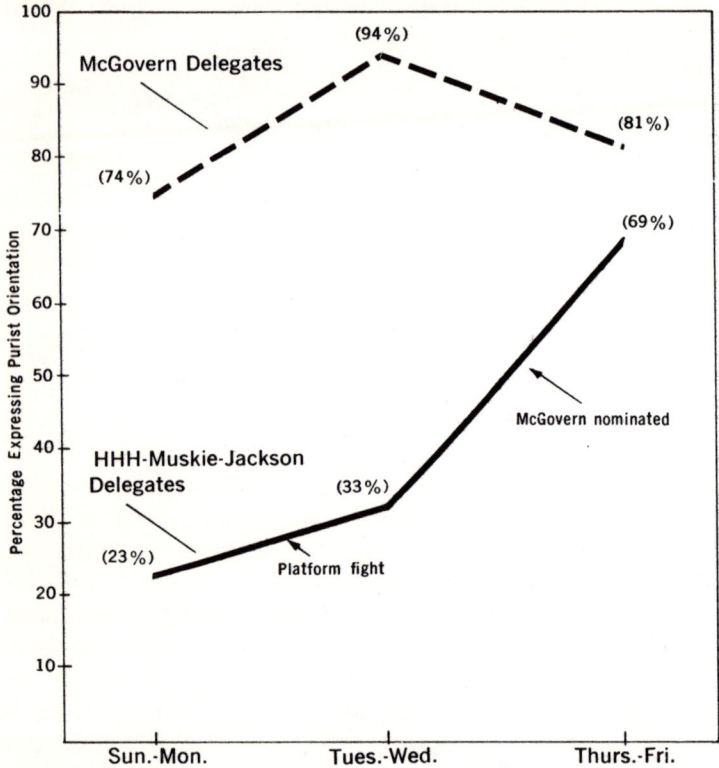

For the HHH group the change in the purist percentage is statistically significant by chi square with probability less than .012. Candidate preference is candidate most preferred at time of interview.

the lead of McGovern in extending those same notions to party unity. If, indeed, McGovern had moved to the center, he had not moved his followers with him. Possibly, the Democratic regulars saw this as a failure of a more fundamental sort. For them, McGovern's movements were almost irrelevant; he was the captive of a new constituency that had taken their party away. As one labor delegate from Pennsylvania remarked to us, McGovern had not depended upon the labor movement for his victory and thus owed labor nothing. For him, McGovern's overtures to labor meant little.

The comments of the Pennsylvania delegate suggest the direction of our findings on the supporters of the losing candidates. If the hypothesis that winning does not convert purists into professionals received little support from our data, the opposite seems to have happened for the losers. Whereas on Sunday and Monday Democratic regulars were thinking as professionals are reputed to think, on Thursday and Friday they were almost as purist as the McGovern supporters. What we seem to see here is a process of radicalization. When party control shifts to an insurgent group, the issues assume as great an importance for the regulars as they formerly held for the purists.

Losers and Legitimation

One of the more celebrated functions of conventions is their legitimation of the Presidential nominee as a candidate that all segments of the party can support.[9] If this result is to be achieved, the winner must take into consideration the vital interests of the losing coalition; in exchange for such consideration the losers pledge themselves to support the winner. If the exchange is successful, it is called party unity, and a presumably unified party can then turn to the task of winning the general election.

If legitimation as we have just described it is to occur, a number of preconditions have to be met. First, the issues that divide winners and losers cannot be of such magnitude that they make each potential compromise seem a betrayal of the vital interests of either coalition. Second, the energy that fuels the process of mutual adjustment and eventual legitimation is the prospect of winning office. Whenever the prospects for winning the general election are poor, the incentive for party unity weakens. Third, and most important in the eyes of some, is the matter of the political style of those who conduct the convention business. Effective politics requires a political style that we have labeled "professional." Those who pursue purist aims in party politics are viewed as disruptive because they prevent the carrying through of "normal politics." The Democratic regulars in 1968 viewed the McCarthyite delegates as "little boys with marbles; you don't play by their rules—they want to break up the game." In the eyes of many Democratic regulars, the 1972 reform rules had produced a convention in which the "little boys" were in command.[10] They had changed the rules of the game and now had all the marbles, or so it seemed. In order to better understand why the convention failed to unify the party around McGovern, let us examine each of the preconditions in more detail.

ISSUE DIFFERENCES BETWEEN MCGOVERN SUPPORTERS AND REGULARS. The issues that divided the two camps were both symbolic and real. McGovern appealed to the idealism of a new young constituency in which moral integrity would replace an older political morality. McGovern would establish new constituencies that would stand alongside the old, and upon which he would depend for support. But differences in style were amplified by differences in substance. On an index of issue liberalism constructed from delegate opinions on busing, amnesty, and guaranteed annual income, we compared McGovern supporters and Democratic regulars supporting Humphrey, Jackson, Muskie." (See Table 6.) McGovern

TABLE 6. Positions of Delegates on Index of Liberalism (Busing, Amnesty, Guaranteed Annual Income), by Candidate Preference

	Lib!!	Lib!	Con!	Con!!	Total
Preference for McGovern	31% (31)	54% (54)	14% (14)	1% (1)	100
Preference for HHH, Muskie, or Jackson	12 (6)	13 (7)	35 (18)	40 (21)	52
Total	24 (37)	40 (61)	21 (32)	15 (22)	152

supporters were decidedly more liberal. The profound differences in both style and substance made the process of mutual adjustment difficult, if not impossible.

THE EXPECTATION OF WINNING IN NOVEMBER. The incentives for party activity revolve around winning and holding elective office. Many observers see the expectation of winning as one of the more powerful forces holding together a party after a bitter nomination fight. But in 1972, expectations about McGovern's chances in the fall election seemed to have played a different role. It must be remembered that McGovern was an insurgent candidate who built a constituency that the party regulars regarded first with indifference and later, as McGovern's power increased, with hostility. The delegates with McGovern at Miami had come a long way without help from the regular party organization. At the convention they saw themselves as winners of the party prize, sure that the same effort would yield the same dividends in November. They were, then, amateur purists who saw no reason for compromise and reconciliation at this late date. When asked by our interviewers about McGovern's chances in the fall election, 72 percent of his supporters thought he was sure to win.[12] Of course, their strong partisan response is partly role expectation; it would be close to treason to admit that one's candidate is a loser. But more important from our point of view, McGovern supporters believed in their candidate and his new politics.

Given the above, then, it should be no surprise that the McGovern delegates maintained their level of purism over the course of the convention. They felt confident in the prospects of victory and sure that the defeated regulars would want to join the victors. The defeated regulars, on the other hand, were just as confident that McGovern was a loser. The 72 percent of the HHH-Muskie-Jackson forces who felt that McGovern was a sure loser in November had little incentive for compromise; for the regulars, the most prudent strategy was to disassociate themselves from McGovern on an issue basis, sit out the election, and pick up the pieces after McGovern was discredited at the polls.[13]

Thus, it seems that a convention divided over the prospects of victory, as well as over substantive issues, polarizes expectations around candidate preference. Partisans of both sides claim their candidate to be a winner, the opponent, a loser. The sharper the issue cleavage in the convention, the stronger the effect of candidate preference on expectations of winning. Thus, in a polarized convention, expectations of winning may well serve to exacerbate conflict, not dampen it.[14]

THE ISSUE OF POLITICAL STYLE. An argument might be constructed that had the McGovern delegates been more political and less purist in their orientations, the prospects of victory in November would have made them more willing to work through the party. It is a trademark of the professional that he sees victory coming through the efforts of a unified party.

Among McGovern's rank-and-file delegates, as distinct from those on the leadership level, we see a number of signs that, if anything, the McGovern delegates thought less of the traditional party on Thursday after the nomination than they did on the previous Sunday. Throughout the convention period we asked delegates what groups they thought of themselves as representing at the convention, and which of these groups were more important to them. We divided the replies into two broad categories; representation of the Democratic rank and file and that of newly organized national constituency groups—youth, women, and blacks. As one might expect, a sense of the efficacy of the new-constituency strategy increased among McGovernites over the course of the convention. While on Sunday and Monday only 47 percent thought of themselves as representing elements of the new constituency, 60 percent thought so on Thursday and Friday.[15] And it was among McGovern supporters who thought of themselves in a new-constituency perspective that the expectation of winning in November was the strongest.[16]

Although McGovern's success in Miami did not modify the attitude of his supporters toward the party in any appreciable sense, some rather startling changes did take place in their attitudes toward the losing candidate. One might expect the victorious purists to despise a defeated rival, but on almost every measure of warmth of feeling for Hubert Humphrey, McGovern supporters showed more toward him on Thursday than on the Monday prior to his withdrawal from the race. It is almost as if those who defeated him could afford to like him. It may be that an increase in affection toward a rival for power is possible only after he has been disarmed. On Sunday and Monday only 13 percent of the McGovern supporters were warm toward Humphrey; by Wednesday evening this figure had risen to 32 percent and by Friday it was 36 percent. It was possible, then, for the purists to disassociate the man from the party.

Let us close this chapter with a look at the delegates who were losers and their styles. In normal political years, the defeated coalition, if it is composed of party professionals, swallows its pride and reconciles itself with the winners in the name of party unity. The losers do so because they are identified with the party and hope to win in November. But, as we have argued, the party regulars this time seemed to become more issue oriented over the course of the convention, and this purism was, in part, a rational response to the political situation.

Many losers expressed the view that the norms of intra-party democracy had been violated in both the selection of delegates and the convention procedures. Like good purists who had been shut out, they demanded a redistribution of power that would enhance their resources. On Monday, only 6 percent of the Humphrey-Jackson-Muskie delegates felt that all important decisions had been made before the convention gathered in Miami; by Friday, 29 percent felt so.[17] There were other signs of disaffection. Although the level of identification with party remained relatively constant among the anti-McGovern regulars, there was a slight decline in this group's warmth of feeling toward the Democratic party.[18] Before the convention opened on Monday, roughly three-quarters of the anti-McGovern regulars felt warm toward the party; by Friday this had declined to little more than 50 percent. It seems that more than just a professional orientation toward politics was needed to unify the party in Miami in 1972.

But the losers did not end their stay at Miami on an acrimonious note. Possibly the willingness of Humphrey, Muskie, and Jackson to join hands with McGovern Thursday night was responsible. Whatever the cause, the anti-McGovern losers confined their antagonisms to McGovern the nominee, and they did not extend them to McGovern the person. Or possibly they had been unusually antagonistic to McGovern on Monday because he was a rival for power. But the data we have accumulated clearly indicates that, over the course of the convention, the response to McGovern as a person grew warmer among the anti-McGovern losers. On Monday, prior to the opening of the convention, only 6 percent of the anti-McGovern regulars felt warm toward McGovern; on the eve of the nomination the figure rose to 21 percent and by Friday it was 47 percent.[19] If one of the functions of a convention is to foster a certain cordiality on the part of the losers toward the winners, then it certainly did so in 1972. This increase may have reflected McGovern's efforts to move to the center in order to unify the party. But if a sense of personal reconciliation was generated by these efforts, it remained confined to the person of McGovern. Possibly, this is all one can hope for from a convention in which the antagonisms were as bitter as they were in Miami in 1972.

NOTES

1. The names I have assigned to the delegates in this section are fictitious, but the profiles come from our interview data and have not been altered in any way. In most cases, I have tried to use interviews in which our interviewers faithfully transcribed the comments of a delegate. In some cases, however, the interviews are paraphrased.

2. Both McGovern and his staff took pains to announce at periodic intervals that they were moving in a centrist direction. In Chapter 4 of this study Benjamin Page discusses the preconvention Platform Committee negotiations from this perspective. A reasonably clear indication of McGovern's concern for the party center came during the credentials challenge of the Chicago Daley delegation and the handling of the platform on the convention floor Tuesday evening.

3. The quotations from interviews should not be seen as supporting the stereotyped view of the McGovern delegate. Many of these delegates were capable of putting first things first, of suppressing notions of issue purity to ensure McGovern's nomination and electoral victory. It would be an oversimplification to say that they were simply engaged in expressive behavior congruent with their notions of themselves as issue purists. For the most part, they tried

to understand the political realities about them and behave instrumentally. But it did seem that the focus for their rational behavior was the McGovern organization, not the party. To compromise in the pursuit of the noble goal of nominating McGovern was one thing; to compromise fundamental issues in the name of party unity and electoral victory may have been simply too much on such short notice.

4. It may be instructive to compare the concept of delegate style with those of ethnocentrism and dogmatism. See, for example, Milton Rokeach, *The Open and Closed Mind* (New York: Basic Books, 1960).

5. James Q. Wilson, *The Amateur Democrat* (Chicago: University of Chicago Press, 1966). See especially Chap. 12, "The New Party Politics: An Appraisal." Political style in the Democratic conventions of 1960 and 1968 and the Republican convention of 1964 is described with insight by Aaron Wildavsky in, *The Revolt Against the Masses* (New York: Free Press, 1971), Chaps. 12–14.

6. John Soule and James Clarke, "Amateurs and Professionals: A Study of Delegates to the 1968 Democratic National Convention," appears in the *American Political Science Review,* vol. 64 (September 1970): 888–99.

7. The percentage of each group expressing a purist orientation is as follows: amateurs, 86% (54); identifiers, 60% (59); regulars, 36% (13). The differences are statistically significant by chi square at less than the .001 level.

8. All the differences between purists and politicians described above are significant by chi square at a probability less than .05.

9. See, for example, V. A. Key, *Politics, Parties, and Pressure Groups,* 6th ed. (New York: Thomas Y. Crowell, 1964), Chap. 15.

10. Wildavsky, *The Revolt Against the Masses,* op. cit., p. 271.

11. The differences in liberalism by candidate preference are statistically significant by chi square at less than the .001 level. The gamma expressing the strength of the relationship is .754.

12. The table relating expectation of McGovern winning in November and candidate preference is reproduced below. It shows almost perfect symmetry.

	Expect McGovern to win	Expect McGovern to lose	Total
Preference for McGovern	73% (87)	27% (33)	120
Preference for HHH, Muskie, or Jackson	28 (23)	72 (60)	83
			203

The probability that the relationship is a chance one is below the .001 level by chi square with 1 degree of freedom. Yules $Q = .746$ indicating a hefty relationship between candidate preference and expectation of victory in November.

13. Note the comments of Capuzzo on page 116.

14. In a convention in which there is a great issue difference, symbolic or real, between rival factions, the tendency seems to be for the party regulars to join the faction closest to their issue position. This, in turn, influences their perceptions of who can win, which in turn may reduce their desire to accommodate to a winner in the event that the party regulars lose. Thus, conventions, and the party regulars who make them work, may have certain constraints on their effectiveness. If the issues are intense, the conventions fail to legitimate; if not, there is little need for legitimation.

15. Although the trend is clear, the differences by time are significant by chi square at the .137 level, a level far too high for safety's sake.

16. The difference is only 8 percent, however, which is not statistically significant.

17. Although the difference seems quite strong, it is statistically significant at the .126 level, again too high for safety's sake.

18. Again, the difference does not approach statistical significance.

19. Statistically significant change over time at the .006 level by chi square.

appendix a

Sampling Procedure

A random sample of delegates was obtained by using a list of delegate names provided to the Dartmouth research group by Ken Bode, Director of the Center for Political Reform. The delegates in this list were ordered by state, and by zip code within each state. Lists of random numbers were generated containing approximately 300 numbers per list. Delegate names were assigned numbers sequentially. Delegate names were entered in our sample when their list number corresponded to one of our random numbers.

A sample of approximately 300 delegates was chosen by using the above procedure prior to the convention. Each interviewer was given 20 cards; each card listed a delegate's name and state. Some of these delegates could not be interviewed because they had not come to Miami or were inaccessible in Miami. On Tuesday, July 11, another sample of approximately 300 delegates was drawn, and each interviewer given another set of 20 cards regardless of the number of interviews completed from the prior set. Interviewers continued to interview delegates listed on the original set of cards. After several unsuccessful attempts to contact a delegate, interviewers were instructed to drop the name.

Although our interviewers were not able to conduct a high percentage of the sample interviews for which they were given cards, the completed interviews do not seem to be a biased sample of the general delegate population. We compared characteristics of delegates in our sample with those of all delegates through the help of data provided by CBS News. For 207 of our respondents we had corresponding data from a CBS study of all delegates. The comparison tests are presented in Table A.1. None of the differences between the total population and our sample is significant.

TABLE A.1

	Difference between poulation mean and sample mean	Probability that difference is *not* significant (t-stat)
Delegate's sex	.014	.70
Delegate's race	.010	.71
Delegate's age	1.21	.19 *
Delegate's education	.028	.61 *
Delegate's occupation	−.028	.93

* Assuming unequal variances.

We are also able to compare our sample to the general population in terms of candidate preference, political experience, and attitudes. Our sample does not differ significantly from the population on any of these variables. Table A.2 summarizes the results of our tests.

Time Distribution of Sample

Much of our analysis is based on the assumption that the samples of delegates interviewed are relatively equivalent each day. Some tests of sample differences by date of interview proved, however, to be statistically significant.

Three delegate groups were delineated according to whether they were interviewed between Sunday morning and Monday evening, Tuesday morning and Wednesday evening, or anytime on Thursday. Delegates interviewed on Friday were left out of much of the analysis because they were found to be largely McGovern delegates.

Each of the three groups of delegates was then tested against the population using the same procedure outlined above. Tests were carried out on nine variables—sex, race,

TABLE A.2

	Difference between population mean and sample mean	Probability that difference is *not* significant (*t*-stat)
Candidate preference	−.11	.75
Public office	−.16	.52
Party office	.012	.92
Number of previous conventions attended	.07	.15
Attitude on busing	.018	.74 *
Attitude on amnesty	.13	.10
Attitude on guarteed income	.01	.80

* Assuming unequal variances.

age, education, occupation, attitude on busing, attitude on amnesty, attitude on guaranteed income, and candidate preference. The results are presented in Table A.3. The figures outside the parentheses are the probabilities that the observed differences between the sample mean and the population mean are significant. The figures within the parentheses are the differences between the two means.

The Sunday–Monday delegate sample is quite representative of their respective population. Excepting race, the population and sample means are not significantly different. The difference in racial composition of the samples is not large. The Tuesday–Wednesday sample of delegates does differ from the population in two ways: our sample is significantly younger than the population and more "liberal" on the three attitude questions. It is possible, then, that the younger, more liberal Tuesday–Wednesday sample may have caused changes over time that are more a result of sampling than of convention dynamics. Luckily, none of our findings is confounded by this.

TABLE A.3. Probability That Difference in Means Is Not Significant *

	Sunday–Monday	Tuesday–Wednesday	Thursday
Delegate's sex	.68	.92	.92
	(.05)	(−.01)	(.01)
Delegate's race	.09 †	.30	.82
	(.05)	(−.05)	(.01)
Delegate's education	.28	.82	.98
	(.10)	(−.02)	(.00)
Delegate's age	.72 †	.00 †	.00 †
	(.54)	(5.02)	(6.78)
Delegate's occupation	.54	.64	.98
	(.63)	(−.50)	(.02)
Attitude on busing	.97	.03	.98
	(.00)	(.25)	(.00)
Attitude on amnesty	.30	.03	.03
	(.15)	(.34)	(.44)
Attitude on guaranteed income	.53	.00	.86
	(.06)	(.24)	(.02)
Candidate preference	.58	.84	.(55)
	(−.41)	(.11)	(−.46)

* The figures in parentheses are the differences between the population means and the sample means.
† Assuming unequal variances.

The Thursday group is also significantly younger than the population. This group, like the Tuesday–Wednesday group, is significantly more "liberal" on the question of amnesty. Unlike the Tuesday–Wednesday group, however, it does not differ significantly in its attitudes on busing or guaranteed income.

On the whole the three groups do not appear to differ from each other in any predictable way over time.

appendix b

Questionnaire

. . . .

The following interview form was used by the Dartmouth–University of California research group at the 1972 Democratic Convention.

1. Interviewer Name_____
2. Date of Interview_____
3. Place of Interview_____
4. Time Interview Started_____
5. Time Interview Completed_____

Interview Guide

1. HOW DO YOU LIKE BEING DOWN IN MIAMI SO FAR? (Probe for delegate's travel to Miami. Friends? Delegation: Travel or stay together?)
   _____
   _____

1a. HOW ARE YOU PLANNING TO SPEND (HAVE YOU BEEN SPENDING) YOUR TIME? (Probe for recreation, political.)
   _____
   _____

1b. IS THIS YOUR FIRST CONVENTION AS A DELEGATE?_____ (if "NO") WHAT?_____YEARS_____

1b1. WHICH CANDIDATE DID YOU SUPPORT IN 1968?
   _____

1c. IN RUNNING FOR DELEGATE, WAS YOUR NAME PUBLICLY ASSOCIATED WITH ANY CANDIDATE? (if "YES") WHO? (Probe for nature and strength of association.)

CANDIDATE_____HOW ASSOCIATED_____
(Probe if necessary to discover present commitments.)

ARE YOU SUPPORTING A PARTICULAR CANDIDATE NOW? WHO? NAME_____

1d. IS THERE ANYTHING THAT MIGHT LEAD YOU NOT TO VOTE FOR_____? (if "YES") WHAT? (Probe for legal obligation, number of ballots committed, second choice.)

1e. DO YOU THINK OF YOURSELF AS REPRESENTING ANY OF THE FOLLOWING GROUPS WHILE YOU ARE HERE AT MIAMI? (Hand delegate group name card.)

PEOPLE WHO VOTED FOR ME	(1) ___
GROUPS SUPPORTING MY CANDIDACY	(2) ___
LABOR	(3) ___
BLACKS	(4) ___
YOUNG PEOPLE	(5) ___
WOMEN	(6) ___
SOUTHERNERS	(7) ___
RANK-AND-FILE DEMOCRATS IN NATION	(8) ___
SUPPORTERS OF MY CANDIDATE IN NATION	(9) ___
RANK-AND-FILE DEMOCRATS IN STATE OR DISTRICT	(10) ___
SUPPORTERS OF MY CANDIDATE IN STATE OR DISTRICT	(11) ___
OTHERS	(12) ___

1f. WHAT GROUP IS MOST IMPORTANT TO YOU? SECOND MOST IMPORTANT?

Appendix B

FIRST_____(Enter number.)
SECOND_____

1g. GENERALLY SPEAKING, DO YOU CONSIDER YOURSELF A DEMOCRAT, INDEPENDENT, OR WHAT? (After answer) ARE YOU A STRONG (   ) OR A NOT STRONG (   )?

STRONG DEMOCRAT_____
NOT STRONG DEMOCRAT_____
NOT STRONG INDEPENDENT_____
STRONG INDEPENDENT_____
OTHER_____

2. HOW ABOUT THE CONVENTION? WHAT IS THE MOST IMPORTANT THING YOU WANT TO SEE DONE HERE?

_____
_____

2a1. WHY IS THAT IMPORTANT TO YOU? (Probe for delegate's underlying goals and relationships among them.)

_____
_____
_____

2a2. HOW DO YOU SEE_____ (describe most important thing) COMING ABOUT? (Probe for delegate perception of outcome certainty.)

_____
_____
_____

2b. WHAT ROLE DO YOU SEE FOR YOURSELF IN BRINGING THIS ABOUT? (Probe for specific activities.)

_____
_____
_____

2c. WHERE DO YOU THINK THE MOST IMPORTANT DECISIONS WERE MADE OR WILL BE MADE CONCERNING_____? (Describe delegate's answer to 2; hand delegate card.)

Black Caucus_____
My state delegation_____
Youth Caucus_____
Labor groups_____
Women's Caucus_____
McGovern candidate organization_____
Wallace candidate organization_____
Humphrey candidate organization_____
Chisholm candidate organization_____
Muskie candidate organization_____
On the convention floor_____
Was all decided before convention_____
(ask) HOW?

_____
_____
_____

2d. DO YOU SEE YOURSELF PARTICIPATING IN THE DELIBERATIONS OF ANY OF THESE GROUPS? (Go over names of groups recording delegate's reaction to each.) If delegate says yes, probe with HOW?

_____
_____

2d1. HOW DO YOU SEE THESE GROUPS RELATING TO_____? (Describe delegate's main goal. Again show card from 2c. Note any group mentioned negatively or positively, and why.)

_____
_____

3. NOW WE'D LIKE YOU TO INDICATE YOUR ATTITUDES TOWARD THESE GROUPS ON WHAT WE CALL A "FEELING THERMOMETER." (Hand dele-

Appendix B

gate feeling thermometer card.) I'LL READ YOU THE NAME OF THE GROUP AND YOU INDICATE HOW WARM OR COLD YOU FEEL TOWARD THE GROUP.

	Degrees	Comments
LABOR AT THE CONVENTION	_____	_____
BLACKS AT THE CONVENTION	_____	_____
YOUTH AT THE CONVENTION	_____	_____
WOMEN AT THE CONVENTION	_____	_____
DEMOCRATIC PARTY	_____	_____
REPUBLICAN PARTY	_____	_____

NOW COULD YOU DO THE SAME THING FOR SOME INDIVIDUALS?

	Degrees	Comments
GEORGE WALLACE	_____	_____
EDWARD KENNEDY	_____	_____
SHIRLEY CHISHOLM	_____	_____
HUBERT HUMPHREY	_____	_____
RICHARD NIXON	_____	_____
WILBUR MILLS	_____	_____
GEORGE MC GOVERN	_____	_____
EDMUND MUSKIE	_____	_____

4. LET'S TURN FOR A MOMENT TO SOME SPECIFIC CONCERNS OF THE CONVENTION. WE MAY HAVE TOUCHED ON SOME OF THESE POINTS ALREADY, BUT WE WANT TO GIVE YOU A CHANCE TO EXPRESS YOUR OPINIONS FULLY.

   WHAT ABOUT THE PLATFORM? WHAT DO YOU WANT (LIKE) IN IT? WHAT DO YOU *NOT* WANT (LIKE) IN IT? (Probe for specifics.)

   _____
   _____
   _____
   _____

   WHY? (Probe for relation to goals, especially winning votes versus being "right.")

   _____
   _____

4a. WHAT KIND OF PERSON WOULD YOU LIKE TO SEE NOMINATED FOR VICE-PRESIDENT? (Probe for name and characteristics.)

WHY? (Probe for balanced ticket, popularity, or qualifications.)

4b. WHAT DO YOU THINK OF THE NEW RULES FOR DELEGATE SELECTION AND PARTY ORGANIZATION?

WHY?

4c. SUPPOSE A NEW ISSUE CAME UP BEFORE THE CONVENTION? WHO WOULD YOU FIND MOST HELPFUL IN DECIDING HOW TO VOTE? (Probe for specific groups, for example, state delegation, named friends, caucus, candidate organization. Record any mention of differences for different kinds of issues.)

WHAT CONSIDERATIONS WOULD BE MOST IMPORTANT TO YOU IN MAKING UP YOUR MIND ON THE ISSUE? (Probe for particular concerns, such as to help blacks help win the election, party unity, nominate a particular candidate.)

5a. LET'S TURN FOR A MOMENT TO THE PRESIDENTIAL NOMINATION. DO YOU THINK MCGOVERN WILL WIN THE NOMINATION? HOW CERTAIN ARE YOU? (Omit this question after nomination.)

Yes, very certain   Yes, not certain   DK (Don't know)
No, not certain   No, very certain

5b. IF MC GOVERN WERE TO WIN THE PRESIDENTIAL NOMINATION, DO YOU THINK HE WOULD WIN THE ELECTION IN NOVEMBER? HOW CERTAIN ARE YOU?

Yes, very certain   Yes, not certain   DK   No, not certain
No, very certain

5c. HOW WOULD MC GOVERN'S NOMINATION AFFECT OTHER NATIONAL AND STATE RACES IN YOUR STATE?

5d. HOW WOULD MC GOVERN'S NOMINATION AFFECT HOUSE AND SENATE RACES ACROSS THE NATION? (Probe for magnitude of effect, for example, would Democrats lose control of the house.)

5e. ARE YOU RUNNING FOR ELECTIVE OFFICE IN NOVEMBER? (If "YES") HOW WOULD A MCGOVERN NOMINATION AFFECT YOUR CANDIDACY?

REMEMBER TO TAKE OUT YOUR ADDRESS BOOK AND RECORD DELEGATE LOCAL ADDRESS, PHONE NUMBER, NAME, AND WILLINGNESS TO BE REINTERVIEWED

NAME OF DELEGATE_____
LOCAL ADDRESS_____
PHONE NUMBER_____
WILLINGNESS TO BE REINTERVIEWED_____
WILLINGNESS TO FILL OUT MAIL
    QUESTIONNAIRE_____
DELEGATE RACE_____
DELEGATE SEX_____
DELEGATE AGE_____

THUMBNAIL SKETCH OF DELEGATE: (Jot down campaign buttons, dress, appearance, style, attitude toward interview, level of knowledge; capture colorful details! Also special circumstances—interviewer knows him well, interview interrupted, and so forth.)

appendix c

Chronology of Convention Events

Sunday, July 9

AFTERNOON

1:30 P.M. Party chairman Lawrence O'Brien issues credentials procedural rulings that bolster McGovern's position.

2:00 P.M. Black Caucus meeting; Presidential candidates appear to ask for support.

Monday, July 10

MORNING

10:00 A.M. McGovern youth meeting; Black Caucus meeting.

AFTERNOON

1:00 P.M. Women's Caucus meeting; Presidential candidates appear.

2:00 P.M. Youth Caucus meeting; attendance is light.

4:00 P.M. Black Caucus meeting.

EVENING

7:00 P.M. Convention session—Credentials. The major credentials challenges begin.

10:50 P.M.	South Carolina challenge—McGovern avoids parliamentary trap.
12:50 A.M.	California challenge—McGovern wins back full delegate slate.
4:00 A.M.	Illinois challenge—Challengers unseat Mayor Daley and his delegates.
4:50 A.M.	Convention session adjourns.

Tuesday, July 11

AFTERNOON

12:00 NOON–1:00 P.M.	Humphrey and Muskie withdraw from contention.
1:00 P.M.	Black Caucus meeting.

EVENING

7:00 P.M.	Convention session—Platform. George Wallace appears before delegates in a wheelchair to urge major changes (most importantly, inclusion of a strong antibusing plank) in the platform. But all major challenges to Platform Committee draft are defeated on convention floor.
6:20 A.M.	Platform adopted.
6:21 A.M.	Session adjourns.

Wednesday, July 12

AFTERNOON	Three hundred demonstrators confront McGovern at Doral Hotel to protest his statement that he would retain military presence in Thailand to secure release of POWs.
3:30–4:00 P.M.	McGovern talks to demonstrators in Doral lobby on national television; Black Caucus meeting.
EVENING	Youth Caucus meeting; large attendance but no significant action.

Appendix C 149

7:00 P.M.	Convention session—Presidential Nomination.
11:58 P.M.	McGovern wins on first ballot, with Jackson finishing second and Wallace third.
12:55 A.M.	Session adjourns.

Thursday, July 13

AFTERNOON

3:30 P.M.	McGovern selects Eagleton as his choice for Vice-President.

EVENING

7:00 P.M.	Convention session—Nomination of Vice-Presidential Candidate and Acceptance Speeches.
1:40 A.M.	Eagleton wins on first ballot, although a number of other candidates receive votes.
2:50 A.M.	McGovern delivers acceptance speech.
3:25 A.M.	Convention adjourns.

Friday, July 14

AFTERNOON	Democratic National Committee meeting: Jean Westwood is elected new DNC chairman, but committee brushes aside Pierre Salinger, McGovern's choice for vice-chairman, and chooses Basil Paterson, a black state legislator, instead.

Index

Abel, I. W., 95
Abernathy, Ralph, 47
Abortion issue, 54, 61
Abzug, Bella, 62
Alternatives '72, 93, 94, 95
Amnesty issue, 32, 87
Axelrod, Robert, 4

Baraka, Imamu, 48, 60
Beck, Audrey, 62
Bie, Norman, 102
Black Caucus, 44-51, 59, 61. *See also* Caucuses
Boggs, Tim, 54, 55
Bond, Julian, 60
Brown, Willie, 47, 48
Busing issue, 31, 32

Candidate organizations, 64-65, 68. *See also* Humphrey; McGovern; Muskie; Wallace organization
Carpenter, Liz, 52
Caucuses, 11-12, 42-43, 44-62, 64, 66, 68; organizational problems of, 58-62, 65. *See also* Black Caucus; Jewish Caucus; Latin Caucus; Senior Citizens' Caucus; Women's Caucus; Youth Caucus
Chavez, Anna, 98, 99
Chisholm Shirley, 44, 46, 50, 53, 60
Clarke, James, 119
Clay, William, 45
Common Cause, 96
Congressional Black Caucus, 12, 44, 60
Convention: caucuses, *See* Caucuses; decision-making, 7-8, 11, 12, 41-43, 44, 45, 52, 56, 93; delegates, *See* Delegates; Events Chronology, 147-

Convention (*cont.*)
49; of states, *See* State conventions; representation, 10, 17-37; structure, 8. *See also* Democratic National Convention

Delegates, 10, 11, 117; and platform committee, 98-99; and platform issues, 30-33, 73, 76-78, 104-107, 110-11; differences among, 33-34; issue-oriented, 119-21, 123-25; McGovern, 128-30; party-oriented, 119-21, 123-25; political experience of, 24-27, 29, 35; questionnaire, 139-46; selection of, 18, 19, 21, 37, 42. *See also* Democratic National Convention; Democratic Party
Democratic National Convention (1968), 4, 27
Democratic National Convention (1972), 5, 9, 27; and the issues, 13; political styles at, 14-15, 122-25, 127, 128, 130-32. *See also* Convention; Delegates; Democratic Party
Democratic Party, 3, 4, 6; drafting the platform of the, 91-105, 110, 111; platform (1972), 13-14, 71, 72-91, 112-13; reform rules, 17-19, 23, 36-37; unity, 116-18, 127-32. *See also* Delegates; Democratic National Convention
Democratic Policy Council, 93, 94
Downs, Anthony, 71-72

Environmental issues, 89
Epps, Ed, 99
Evers, Charles, 48

Farenthold, Frances ("Sissy"), 54, 87

151

Index

Farmer, Joe, 54, 55, 56
Fauntroy, Walter, 45, 50, 59, 60
For the People, 78. *See also* Democratic Party, platform

Gibson, Kenneth, 91, 98, 103
Goldwater, Barry, 19, 21
Gregory, Dick, 50
Group quotas. *See* Quota system
Guaranteed annual income issue, 32, 33
Gunter, Annie, 102

Hatcher, Richard, 48, 50
Holum, John, 55
Humphrey, Hubert, 47, 53, 93, 101
Humphrey organization, 10, 61

Jackson, Henry, 104
Jewish Caucus, 57-58. *See also* Caucuses

Kaden, Lewis, 100
Kennedy, Edward, 21

Labor, 95-96
Latin Caucus, 57, 61, 88. *See also* Caucuses
Lyons, John, 10

McCloskey, Herbert, 30, 31
McGovern, George, 18, 21-23, 51, 102, 104; at caucus meetings, 46-47, 52-53; campaign of, 108-110, 113-14, 126, 130-32
McGovern-Fraser Reform Commission, 6, 8
McGovern organization, 10, 19, 27, 124; and the caucuses, 60, 61; and the platform, 13, 14, 87, 100, 101, 107-108; importance of, 64, 68
MacLaine, Shirley, 100
Maloney, J. P., 22
Medical care issue, 80, 84
Muskie, Edmund, 46, 93, 101
Muskie organization, 10

National Black Political Convention, 12, 44, 60
National Women's Political Caucus, 51
Neustadt, Richard E., 91, 97, 98, 99, 100
New Democratic Coalition, 97

O'Brien, Lawrence, 55, 56, 93
Organized labor, 95-96

Page, Benjamin, 13

Party platforms, 72-75. *See also* Democratic Party, platform (1972)
Paterson, Basil, 51
Platform 1972, 97
Platforms, 72-75. *See also* Democratic Party, platform (1972)
Political parties, 1-2
Political roles, 119-23, 124
Political style, 14-15, 122-25, 127, 128, 130-32
Polsby, Nelson, 7
Pomper, Gerald, 74
Pressman, Jeffrey, 11, 12
Primaries, 22

Quota system, 10-11, 17, 18, 27, 33; effects of the, 29, 35-37

Republican Party, 7
Rockefeller, Nelson, 21

Salinger, Pierre, 51
Sanford, Terry, 46, 53
School busing. *See* Busing issue
Segal, Eli, 55
Senior Citizens' Caucus, 57. *See also* Caucuses
Slate-making. *See* Delegates, selection of; Quota system
Slocombe, Walter, 100
Soule, John, 119
State conventions, 19
State delegations, 41-43, 62-64, 68. *See also* Delegates
Stearns, Rick, 55
Stokes, Louis, 45
Sullivan, Denis, 10, 14, 15

Tax reform issue, 84

United Farm Workers, 96
Unit rule, 42

Van Dyk, Ted, 101, 102
Vietnam war issue, 82
Voting patterns, 4, 6

Wallace, George, 21, 22, 49, 101-102
Wallace organization, 13
Wall Street Journal, 84
Wildavsky, Aaron, 7, 119
Wilson, James Q., 119
Women's Caucus, 51-54, 61, 62. *See also* Caucuses

Youth Caucus, 54-57, 62. *See also* Caucuses

Zeidman, Philip, 100